Keys to Joy

How to Unlock God's Gift of Lasting Happiness

Gaylyn R. Williams

Ken Williams, Ph.D.

Relationship Resources, Inc.

Colorado Springs, CO

Published by Relationship Resources, Inc.

Contact Relationship Resources for additional copies and quantity discounts:

    PO Box 63383, Colorado Springs, CO 80962

    www.RelationshipResources.org;

    email: info@RelationshipResources.org

Library of Congress Control Number: 2012910761

Paperback ISBN: 9780972172882

Endorsements

"John records a wonderful statement made by Jesus, "I have told you these things so that you will be filled with my joy. Yes, your joy will overflow! (John 15:11 NLT) Jesus wants our joy to overflow. What are these things that Jesus spoke of? In this book, *Keys to Joy*, Ken and Gaylyn Williams, the father-daughter writing team, do us a favor by reminding us of the things that lead to joy in the Christian life. Based on the study of God's Word, the contents of this book will lead the reader to a greater sense of who God is, and a deep abiding peace in the One who loves us and wants a relationship with his children.

Bob Creson
President/CEO of Wycliffe Bible Translators USA

In the midst of a world filled with broken promises and elusive dreams, *Keys to Joy* provides powerful clarity to obtaining lasting joy. Each chapter contains poignant narrative packed with spiritual truth and practical application. Everyone desires joy, but few discover the key to obtaining it. *Keys to Joy* unlocks the mystery of joy's obscurity by providing 12 surprising truths. It's a must read for every avid "joy" seeker.

Julie Gorman
FYI Founder and Executive Director

Joy is one of the fruits of the spirit which I find so challenging to allow to grow in my life, especially during times of uncertainty and pain. Guilt and condemnation seem to follow during these difficult times. With much hope, Gaylyn and Ken, share not only their personal struggles on their journey to joy, but practical steps to allow joy to flourish in even the most challenging times.

Evelyn Sherwood
Ministry Leader, Minister's Wife, Mother, and Grandmother

"The choice to rejoice." That phrase reverberates in my heart since reading this delightful, scriptural study on the keys to Joy. Ken and Gaylyn share personal experiences and give practical, biblical advice (keys) to help believers unlock the door to true joy.

Steven Sherwood Sr.
Pastor of Fairview Baptist Church

Table of Contents

Dedication

To all our ministry partners who have so faithfully
supported us, our families and our ministries
prayerfully and financially.

Thank you. We appreciate you.
We couldn't have written this book without you.

Foreword by Laura Mae Gardner

The privilege of writing this foreword is a precious one. Writing as co-authors—a father-daughter writing team—has its own challenges, but Ken and Gaylyn have managed that beautifully. And they've done it well.

Their topic is so timely, God's Word for believers for this day and this time.

Joy. How much we want it! How much we yearn for it! But it seems elusive and theoretical. Ken and Gaylyn show us that it has the stuff of daily life in it.

Joy is not just for eternity or for Sunday, or for a special few. It's for today, for every day. And it's for all. And they give us the keys to unlock that door.

This book is:

- Eminently practical

- Thoroughly Biblical

- Thirst-promoting

It fills me with eagerness to study it more and enthusiastic about promoting it. It is a super book!!!! I can't say enough good things about it.

Ken and his wife, Bobbie have been a significant part of my husband's and my life for 40 years. Their influence, wisdom and modeling have touched many, many lives, including ours.

Gaylyn is their oldest daughter. She has been active in ministry with Wycliffe Bible Translators, the Navigators and now is the Executive Director of Relationship Resources. She is a gifted woman, whose gifts have been matched by great suffering.

Gaylyn and Ken speak and write with candidness and dignity about the low places in their lives—times of discouragement and despair, of great loss and sadness. They also speak of the joy that sustained them during those times.

Knowing the authors and their lives makes this book ring with authenticity. They've been in the dark places. They've been sustained by God's Word, by Scriptural truths and principles. And they have learned about joy, and practice it. This isn't theoretical for either one of them. It is deep observations and commitments bathed in the waters of suffering.

In this book they have presented those truths in formats and with exercises that are easy to grasp, and practice. This book has the power to change lives of those readers who take it seriously.

I recommend this book and hope it has a permanent place on your book shelves and beside your devotional chair.

"Your principles have been the music of my life throughout the years of my pilgrimage" (Psalm 119:54, TLB). Ken and Gaylyn will turn the concepts about joy into music for your journey too.

Dr. Laura Mae Gardner
International Training Consultant for Wycliffe Bible Translators

Introduction

With one phone call, in an instant my (Gaylyn's) life plunged from giddy happiness to devastating grief.

A week later, I lay curled in my bed sobbing, barely able to catch my breath. Storm clouds shrouded Pikes Peak that July afternoon. Thunder crashed nearby. I wondered, *How can I go on? Another loss. But this is so much worse than all the rest.*

As if from a long way away, I heard my eleven year-old son whimper, "I'm hungry, Mommy."

"I'm so sorry," was all I could say. I knew his heart was also breaking, but I couldn't force myself to get up.

The storm raging outside my window seemed to mirror my life. Just one week earlier, my life was filled with excitement, joy, hope, and more happiness than I had ever experienced. But that day, through the wracking sobs, I started thinking about all the losses I had endured. I cried, "God, why is everything important to me always taken away?"

My first great loss came when I was just six years old when I was left at a boarding school in Guatemala. (My parents grieved too, but it was their only option, because of their work in a remote village.) I was there for eight years, only seeing them on vacations. When I was seven, my close friend died tragically in a raging river.

After college, I married and became a Bible translator. But my struggles had just begun. Nine years into a difficult marriage, my second son was born with numerous problems. He only lived six short months. (I'll share more about him in chapter nine.)

Seven years later my turbulent marriage ended in divorce, and I found myself struggling to raise two rambunctious sons alone. Tears and heartache over my oldest son's destructive choices filled many of those years. I often felt inundated with life.

Finally, after years filled with losses and hardships, my life appeared to make a U-turn. I fell in love with a wonderful man, Ian. Then one month before we were to be married, I received that devastating phone call. Ian had just been killed on his motorcycle.

"No! No! It can't be!"

My life shattered once again. I was besieged by grief. It took every ounce of my energy just to get out of bed. I often wanted to give up. I just wanted to go be with Ian.

Through the dark nights filled with heartbroken sobs, God brought comfort through verses I had memorized, such as "Peace I leave with you, my peace I give to you.... Let not your heart be troubled" (John 14:27).

Reading the Word, praise and prayer helped me focus on the Lord and find my strength in Him. The process was slow. Sometimes I wasn't sure that God even cared about me. Eventually, I began to feel God's peace surround me, like a warm blanket on a winter night.

I knew Philippians 4:4 says, "Rejoice in the Lord always," but I wondered, *how can I have joy when my heart was breaking?*

During the months that followed, I had to make the moment-by-moment choice to focus on the Lord, despite my pain and heartache, even when I didn't feel like it. It wasn't easy and I didn't always succeed. But as I chose to focus on who God is and what He's done, I began to experience joy again (Psalm 16:11).

Joy is a choice for all of us. It's not easy, especially when the hard times pummel us.

Storms still come and go. Whenever I focus on the storms, they can appear overwhelming. But when I gaze instead at my Father who loves me, I begin to have peace and joy. I may not understand why things happen, but I know I can embrace God's love and trust his plans for me, no matter what the future holds. And so can you.

Looking for Joy?

Join the crowd. Everyone searches for joy. Many seek it through health clubs, work, success, money, material possessions, and relationships, yet they discover that "things" don't bring joy. Life's struggles rob many of this mysterious fruit of the Spirit (Galatians 5:22). Consistent joy is a choice made moment-by-moment through application of clear biblical principles.

Keys to Joy is a practical Bible study to help you discover and maintain true joy. This study presents twelve keys to Christian joy. These keys come from the hundreds of references to joy in the Bible and deal with three major relationships—God, others, and ourselves.

Our study uncovers various areas that lock this door. It then offers practical suggestions to unlock it and keep it open. The principles come from what we have both learned to apply from the Word in our lives—especially in the difficult times.

Each chapter contains two sections. The first section, "Discovering the Key," explains the specifics about the key to joy and gives personal illustrations. The stories in these are written by Ken, unless otherwise noted.

The second section of each chapter, "Opening the Door to Joy," is a personal Bible study to help you dig into the Scriptures for yourself. The questions in this study are designed to help you discover the content and meaning of the Scriptures while providing ways to practically apply it to your life.

In 1993 we wrote a book called *The Door to Joy.* Parts of this book are taken from that one. In the years since we wrote that, we have both continued in our quest to use our keys to joy. It's a challenge for us, as it is for most—if not all—people. Our enemy does not want us to experience joy. He does not want us to grow in our relationship with the Lord. He wins if he can keep us focused on our circumstances, rather than on the Lord and on using our keys to joy.

We want to challenge you not to give up, even if joy seems elusive. It's equally available to all of us.

As you begin this study, we pray God will daily increase your joy.

Ken and Gaylyn Williams
a father-daughter writing team

How to Use This Book

This book can be used either alone, with a group or with one other person. We encourage you to study the materials on your own first, and then find at least one other person to study with. Sharing insights together will enhance your learning.

1. Before you begin studying each day, ask God to open your mind and give you insights into His Word. Ask Him to help you apply what you learn.

2. Do your study using a good modern translation of the Bible. Use other translations for a better understanding and clarification of the concepts presented. The questions were written using the *New International Version* (NIV). *The Living Bible* (TLB) and the *Revised Standard Version* (RSV) are referred to.

3. Use a standard dictionary or Bible dictionary to help understand meanings of words.

4. Some questions have many verses listed, and we encourage you to study them all to get a full understanding of the Scriptures. However, if time is limited, at least look at one or two verses for each question.

5. Each chapter includes "Challenge" questions for advanced students or those with extra time. They are designed to increase your understanding of the key to joy, but they are optional. If you don't have time to study the "Challenge" questions as you go through the book, we'd encourage you to come back to them later.

6. Each chapter also includes "Journal" questions to help you dig deeper. They are designed to help you personalize and apply the lesson. Use another page–or a separate journal–if you need more space.

7. Write your answers in the space provided in the study. If you need more space for the "Journal" and "Challenge" questions, as well as any extra studies you would like to do, use a separate notebook or journal. Blank pages are included in the back of this book for your use.

8. If you are studying this book with a group, come to the study session prepared, and willing to share what you've learned. Then listen to what others have learned to increase the benefits of your search for joy.

9. A leader's guide is included at the end of the study. It contains guidelines for the leader's preparation and specific questions to highlight during the Bible study. We find joy, not by seeking it, but by using the keys found in Scripture and identified in this book. Study each chapter with an open mind and eagerly find your joy.

CHAPTER 1

Finding Joy's Door

Discovering the Key

A group of army recruits marched around the base. Suddenly one broke away from the formation, and ran to a nearby door and opened it. "That's not it!" he cried and got back into line. Every time the formation passed a door, he broke rank, flung the door open, and, with great frustration, exclaimed, "That's not it!"

Finally the drill sergeant could take no more. He discussed the situation with the lieutenant, and they decided to send the soldier to the psychiatrist. In the medical office building, he ran down hallway after hallway opening every door, yelling, "That's not it! That's not it!"

After two weeks of intense observation, the psychiatrist told the man, "I'm sorry, but we're discharging you from military service. You have serious problems." After the doctor gave the man his discharge papers, he said, "You're free to go." Opening the outside door, the man shouted, "This is it!"

People are looking everywhere for joy's door. They try one thing then another, thinking, "Maybe this is it." They discover that it doesn't satisfy, so they try something else, only to realize, "That's not it."

After years of seeking joy in the wrong places, when I found Jesus Christ, my heart cried out, "This is it! He is the One I've been looking for all my life." For true joy, He's the only source.

As I followed Christ, I discovered joy is somewhat elusive. Even though I had wonderful joy in Jesus, it was like the sunshine on a cloudy day—shining brightly at times, but sadly missing and longed for at other times. Sometimes joy flows from us like a gushing spring, but much of the time we must hold on for dear life.

In his article, "Joy: The Illusive Fruit," Joe Aldrich (1985) said, "It takes time, diligence, patience and hard work to make an apple tree productive. Fruit is not instantaneous! It is a victory over weather, bugs, weeds, poor soil and neglect. If the Spirit's indwelling presence guaranteed the presence of joy, every believer would be rejoicing all the time. We're not. Joy, as a way of living, is a hard-won victory over entrenched attitudes of apathy, pessimism, doubt, unbelief and despair."

Joy is one of God's highest priorities for us. The Bible mentions it nearly six hundred times! I think the Lord talks about it so much because He really wants us to be filled with joy. He longs for us to live joy-filled lives!

Just what is this joy we're talking about? God's view of joy is very different from the world's view. Calvin Miller said in *The Taste of Joy*, "Many Christians confuse happiness with joy as did I. Happiness is a buoyant emotion that results from the momentary plateaus of well-being. Joy is bedrock stuff. Joy is a confidence that operates irrespective of our moods. Joy is the certainty that all is well, however we feel." (Miller, 1983).

Joy isn't the momentary happiness we feel when everything goes right and problems are at a minimum. It doesn't matter what's happening in our lives. We can still have joy because it isn't a feeling based on circumstances. Joy is an attitude based on our relationship with God.

Some people hold onto a myth—if we're not joyful *every* mznute of *every* day, we're terrible Christians. That myth can rob us of the little joy already in our lives! Every Christian struggles with a lack of joy at times, and I'm convinced that God's response is compassion, not anger. Our hope is that this study will help you become more consistently joyful in your walk with the Lord.

We can choose joy! Think about that for a minute. If God commands joy, then it must be possible to choose it. We can't make it appear magically with a snap of the fingers. But, we can determine to make joy an increasingly more important part of our lives. Each time we make a choice to rejoice, it becomes easier.

Recently I went through a severe struggle. One morning I woke up feeling overwhelmingly discouraged, so I turned to the Psalms for comfort. I "happened" to turn to Psalm 43:4 in the *Revised Standard Version*, "[You are] my exceeding joy." I exclaimed, "Wow, Lord! You don't just give joy. You are my joy! And You are not my common everyday joy, either. *You* are my exceeding Joy." In every spare moment that day, I thanked Him for being my true joy. And my discouragement? It evaporated as the warmth of God's joy flooded over me. It's hard to hold on to discouragement when we fill our thoughts with thrilling truths from God's Word.

It's wonderful to know that we can make a choice to rejoice. In *The Practice of Godliness*, Jerry Bridges says (1996), "The choice is ours. We can be joyless Christians or we can be joyful Christians. We can go through life bored, glum and complaining, or we can rejoice in the Lord. It is both our privilege and our duty to be joyful. To be joyless is to dishonor God and to deny His love and control over our lives. It is practical atheism."

In Philippians 3:1, Paul made a fascinating statement, "My brothers and sisters, rejoice in the Lord! . . . It is a safeguard for you." At first I wondered what that meant. How could joy be a safeguard? Then I realized the danger of being a joyless Christian. When we lose our joy we're vulnerable to what I call "the devil's D's": doubt, discouragement, disillusionment, dejection, depression, despair, and finally, disaster! It should frighten us when we've lost our joy, because our safeguard against the enemy is broken down. Remember, we have a choice to rejoice.

This Bible study will cover twelve keys to joy. First let's look at the Master Key: "Rejoice in the Lord." In Philippians 4:4 Paul says, "Rejoice in the Lord always." When I don't feel like it, I wish he had said, "Rejoice in the Lord sometimes, or when you feel like it." But he says *always*. And then Paul says, "I will say it again: Rejoice!" The Lord is serious in His desire that we rejoice in Him, especially when we don't feel like it.

I wondered what "In the Lord" really meant, so I looked it up in Bible commentaries. They said it meant: in God's love and grace, in fellowship with the Lord, and in knowing God's authority over our lives and our destiny. What a great encouragement this definition is to me! It tells me that joy comes as we snuggle into the arms of our loving, caring, and all-powerful Father who has everything under control. This quality of joy could never be found in mere circumstances.

Joy in the Lord isn't a one-way street. When we're snuggled in His arms, the Lord rejoices over us, too, and sings us a love song. Zephaniah 3:17 says, "The Lord your God is with you, he is mighty to save. He will take great delight in you, he will quiet you with his love, he will rejoice over you with singing."

Consider this awesome reality! The God who created the universe is delighting in you right now with great joy. As He quiets your heart with His love, He bursts into song! Don't you catch the excitement? Maybe you're thinking. *That was for Israel, not for us.* According to Galatians 6:16, we are "the Israel of God." How much more does God rejoice over His beloved children, purchased with His Son's own blood!

God *wants* you to find the door to joy, but you must search in the right place. True joy is found only in your relationship to the Lord. Through the rest of this study you'll be given keys to open that door to joy. To have the fullest joy, you need to learn to use each key.

Opening the Door to Joy

Day 1

1. Read "Discovering the Key."

   a. List any new truths you uncovered.

   b. What will you choose to apply from this section?

2. Write your personal definition of joy.

   What difference do you see between happiness and joy?

3. How does the world search for joy? How successful are they?

   a. According to Job 20:5, how long does worldly joy last?

   b. List the places King Solomon searched for meaning and joy in Ecclesiastes 1:13-14 and 2:1-11.

c. What did he say about his search? Ecclesiastes 1:14; 2:lb, 11b.

4. According to the following Scriptures, where do we find joy's door?

I Samuel 2:1

Job 33:26

Psalm 16:11

5. Journal: List where you have searched for joy. Did you find it? If not, do you know why?

What could you do today to become more joyful?

Meditate on Psalm 16:11. Record how this verse speaks to you.

Day 2

1. What do Psalm 13:5 and Luke 10:20 say we are to rejoice in?

    a. Do you rejoice in those things? Why or why not?

    b. How do these verses affect you today?

2. Without believing in Jesus and trusting Him for our salvation, we will never find true joy. What do the following verses say to you?

    Romans 3:23

    Romans 6:23

    John 3:16

    Romans 10:9-10

    a. If you haven't trusted Jesus, you can invite Him to come into your heart right now using the following prayer: *Dear Lord, I'm a sinner and need You. Please forgive my sins and make me a new person. Take over my life today. Thank You for sending Jesus to die for me. In Jesus' name. Amen.*

    b. What does Luke 15:7 say happens in heaven the moment we put our trust in Jesus?

    c. How do you respond to that?

    d. If you just prayed this prayer, we'd love to hear, so we can pray for you and encourage you. Email us at joy@RelationshipResources.org.

3. Read Acts 16:25-34. What can we learn about joy from the Philippian jailer's response in verse 34?

4. Name one result of believing in Jesus. 1 Peter 1:8

    Meditate on that verse. If you haven't experienced this result, ask the Lord to reveal why you haven't.

5. Write a prayer of thanks to the Lord for your salvation.

6. Journal: List one or two friends who are searching for joy in the wrong places. What specific things can you do to help them find it?

Day 3

1. What do Psalm 32:11 and 81:1 command us to do?

2. Over thirty commands in Scripture are given to rejoice and be glad. Why do you think God commands it so often?

3. Challenge: List other commands to rejoice or to be glad, with their references.

   What is God saying to you through these directives?

4. Who are we to rejoice in and why? See Psalm 97:12; Isaiah 61:10.

   How do these verses impact you today?

5. List things in your relationship to the Lord that bring you joy.

6. Journal: Meditate on your list from question 5. How do these bring you joy today? If they don't, why do you think they don't?

Day 4

1. What do these verses teach about how we should rejoice?

   Zephaniah 3:14

   Zechariah 9:9

   Luke 6:23

2. How much joy does John 17:13 say God wants us to have? (See NIV or TLB.)

   a. Are you experiencing as much joy as God wants you to have? Explain.

b. What do you need to do to have more of it today?

3. Read Philippians 4:4 and 1 Thessalonians 5:16.

   a. How often are we to be joyful?

   b. How often are you joyful?

   c. If there is a discrepancy between 3a and b, what might need to change?

4. How does Psalm 43:4 describe God?

   How is this significant to you?

5. According to Psalm 126:2-3, what fills us with joy and gladness?

6. On a separate paper, or a blank page at the end of this book, list some of the things God has done for you and given you that fill you with joy. Keep this list handy so you can add to it. Whenever you feel discouraged, read through it and be reminded of all He has done.

7. Journal: Write a love note to God thanking Him for all He's done for you and all the joy He has given you.

Day 5

1. Review this study. What will help you find joy's door?

2. What keeps joy's door closed for you?

   What can you do to open it more?

3. Meditate on and memorize a verse from this lesson that will help you find more joy. Write out the verse below.*

   How can you make this truth come alive for you?

4. Journal: Write a prayer of commitment to follow through on what you learned in this study. Record any new insights the Lord gave you.

* For ideas on memorizing Scripture, go to www.365NamesofGod.com.

CHAPTER 2

Knowing God Unlocks Joy

Discovering the Key

Several years ago I tried something that changed my life. While Bobbie and I were on a year-long mission trip, I decided to read only the Bible. No magazines or books for the whole year! The Bible became my source of relaxation on cold nights, my light reading, my study resource, even my only counseling textbook.

My purpose was to know God on a deeper level. I thought, "At the end of this year I'm really going to know God." How naive I was! By the year's end my quest to know the Lord had just begun, but my life had been revolutionized.

Reading through the whole Bible, I made notes on my discoveries about God— who He is and what He's like. Each time I found a new truth, I thanked Him for it and meditated on it until it became a part of me. Then I read through the Bible again, looking at what God has done, is doing, and will do for His people.

This experience drew me into a deep, intimate relationship with God and brought great joy to my life. I challenge you to try it. It might change your life too!

I relate this experience to illustrate the first key to unlocking joy in our lives—a growing "heart knowledge" of God. The more intimately we know God, the greater our joy. This is so essential that all other keys to joy depend on it.

When we hear the word "knowledge" we usually think of facts, figures, and ideas. Our culture teaches us to focus on head knowledge. When the Bible speaks of knowing God, it always means experiential or "heart knowledge."

Did you know that the world's deepest chasm is only fourteen inches—from the head to the heart? Our challenge is to get facts about God down into our heart where they have impact. We must do it if we want to reach into the depths of our Lord's resources.

In 2 Peter 1:3 we read, "His divine power has given us *everything* we need for a godly life *through our knowledge of him* who called us by his own glory and goodness" (italics added for emphasis). Peter is talking about heart-knowledge here, not simply facts about God.

Studying facts about God is a critical first level. But if we want to know Him personally and intimately, we can't remain there. Facts alone can't bring joy in hard times.

How do we get these truths about God down into our hearts? Here are a few ideas. Try each one and add your own favorites to this list.

1. Focus on what God has done and is doing in your life and thank Him.

2. Browse through the Psalms. As you discover descriptions of God, underline them. Then praise Him for who He is.

3. Personalize Scripture by inserting your name in places where pronouns or other nouns are used in the text. Begin with Ephesians 1 and 2.

4. Discover verses that describe God, and memorize them.

5. Meditate on Scripture: Think about it, ask questions about it, consider what God is saying to you personally.

6. Sing praise and worship songs from your heart, focusing on the Lord.

7. Share with others what God reveals to you about Himself.

8. Claim God's promises in tough times. For example, say, "Lord, I don't feel like it, but you said you will never forsake me. So I'm holding on to that."

9. Pray through Scripture. Talk to God about what He is saying to you through the passage and your response to it. Ask the Holy Spirit to interpret for you.

Take a moment to consider these ideas. Which have you tried? What happened? Which can you try this week? God is eager to give you joy. The key is growing more intimate in your knowledge of Him.

Become an expert at bridging the fourteen-inch chasm between your heart and head with God's Word. Discover your favorite skills at doing this, and learn to apply them consciously so truths become more than mere facts.

In 2 Peter 3:18 we're commanded to "grow in the grace and knowledge of our Lord and Savior Jesus Christ." The tense of the Greek word "grow" indicates an ongoing process—we must keep growing in our knowledge of Him.

Continual growth in knowing the Lord takes work! But it's worth the labor. As our "heart-knowledge" of the Lord deepens, we're able to trust Him more, and enjoy His power, goodness, and grace.

What child will crawl up into the lap of a stranger and feel comforted? But imagine the joy in that child's face as she nestles snugly in the familiar arms of her loving father. She can trust him because she knows him so well. It's the same with our Lord. Our trust in Him grows as we come to know Him better.

Colossians 1:10-12 links knowing the Lord and joy. Paul prayed the believers would be "growing in the knowledge of God," and "giving joyful thanks to the Father." We're able to joyfully give thanks to our Father as we come to know Him and all He means to us.

Remember, this process isn't something we can do on our own. The Holy Spirit must be in partnership with us. Jesus gave us His Spirit to help us know Him better. John 14:26 says that the Holy Spirit is our Counselor who will teach us all things.

Since the Spirit is teaching us, can we put the Bible under our pillow, lay back, and say, "O Lord, fill my heart with a knowledge of You?" No! We must be actively involved. We choose how deeply we get to know God. It is possible to remain on an acquaintance level, learning only facts about God. God wants us to know Him and experience joy, but He won't coerce us into a deeper relationship with Him.

When I took a whole year to get to know God, I thought that would do the job. But coming to a deep "heart-knowledge" of the Lord is a lifetime process. When we get to heaven, we will know Him completely—then "we shall be like him, for we shall see him as he is" (1 John 3:2). In the meantime, we can daily choose to know Him in an increasingly deeper way. In the process our joy will grow.

Throughout this study, our hope is that you will grow in a deeper knowledge of God—not just with more facts in your head, but with life-changing truth in your heart. If you haven't made a commitment to grow to know God personally, we urge you to stop right now and do it.

We pray "that the God of our Lord Jesus Christ, the glorious Father, may give you the Spirit of wisdom and revelation, so that you may know him better" (Ephesians 1:17).

Gaylyn is writing a blog, www.DailyNameofGod.com It is designed to help you grow to know God more intimately. Each day gives a different name of the Lord, with one or more Scriptures and some ideas on how to understand or use the name to praise God. You can sign up to get the names in your email each day. She also wrote a new book called *The Surprising Joy of Exploring God's Heart: A Daily Adventure with 365 of His Names*. You can learn more at www.365NamesofGod.com.

Opening the Door to Joy

Day 1

1. Read "Discovering the Key."

    a. List any new truths you uncovered.

    b. What will you apply from this section?

2. Read Hosea 6:1-3. If we have a strained relationship with the Lord, what should be our response? See verse 1.

    a. Can a full measure of joy be found without this response? Explain.

    b. If your relationship with God has grown cold, ask the Lord to forgive you for moving away from Him.

3. What does Hosea 6:3 say we are to do?

    a. From this week's lesson, list a few practical ways to do this.

    b. What does God promise to do when we obey Him?

4. What are some ways we lose our joy?

5. How do we gain joy? Job 33:26; Acts 2:28

    a. How do these things fill you with joy?

    b. If they don't fill you with joy, why not?

6. Go to www.DailyNameofGod.com to sign up to get the daily name.

7. Journal: Evaluate your relationship with the Lord.

    a. Are you growing daily in your knowledge of Him? List ways you are now growing.

    b. Where would you like to be in your relationship with God?

    c. Write one or two specific, attainable goals to help you get there.

Day 2

1. List the actions suggested in the following verses. As you do so, meditate on the verse and ask yourself if you are doing what it says.

   Psalm 105:4

   Isaiah 55:6

   Colossians 3:1-2

   Hebrews 12:2-3

2. What are some results of seeking God? How have you experienced them? If you haven't experienced them, why do you think you haven't? Write down your results and your experience.

   Psalm 34:10

   Psalm 70:4

   Proverbs 8:17

   Jeremiah 29:13

3. Challenge: List other results of seeking God, with Scriptures, if possible.

4. How does Psalm 63:1, and 119:2 and 10 say we are to seek God?

   Do you seek God and long for Him as the psalmist describes the process? Explain.

5. How is seeking God with our minds different from seeking with our hearts?

6. When we read or study the Bible, we have it in our minds. List ways you are moving the truths about God from your head to your heart.

7. Journal: What barriers prevent your seeking God?

    How can you remove them? List specific steps.

Day 3

1. On a separate page, list at least five characteristics that describe the Lord. Meditate on each, and use them to worship God. Each time you discover a new quality, add it to your list.

2. Challenge: Add ten to fifteen characteristics of Jesus to your list.

3. Read John 10:1-16, 25-27. What do you learn about Jesus and your relationship to Him in verses 4, 14, and 27?

    a. How do we learn to know our Shepherd's voice?

    b. What could you do to know His voice better?

    c. What insights do you gain from Proverbs 8:30?

4. Challenge: List ways Jesus is like a Shepherd and we are like sheep. What does He do for His sheep? Support your answers with Scriptures, when possible.

5. Journal: What did Jesus say to the Pharisees in John 8:19?

   Could He say this about you today? If so, what can you do about it?

Day 4

1. Not only do we know God, but also God knows us. What do the following verses say about this?

   Job 23:10

   Psalm 44:21

   Psalm 94:11

   Psalm 103:14

   2 Timothy 2:19

2. How does it make you feel when you begin to understand the depth of God's knowledge about you?

3. How does having a growing heart-knowledge of God bring joy in your life?

4. Read Philippians 3:8-10. What was Paul's greatest desire?

    How is everything else described?

5. Journal: What keeps you from the same commitment Paul had?

    a. What needs to change in your life?

    b. Write Philippians 3:8-10 in your own words as a prayer.

Day 5

1. Review this study. What did you learn that will help unlock your joy?

2. In what ways can knowing God unlock your joy?

3. What did you choose to apply to your life this week? How will you apply it?

4. Meditate on and memorize a verse from this lesson that will help you find more joy. Write out the verse below.

What will you do to make this truth come alive for you?

5. Journal: Record any new insights the Lord gave you in this lesson.

Write a prayer of commitment to follow through on what you learned.

CHAPTER 3

God's Word Reveals Joy

Discovering the Key

The greatest joy of our lives came when we translated God's Word for the Chuj (pronounced "chew") people in the remote mountains of Guatemala. Seeing the Chuj Christians' ravenous hunger for the meat of God's Word changed our lives. As each newly translated portion came off the press, readers gobbled up every word.

The day before the dedication of the complete New Testament in 1970, one young believer joyfully burst out, "Just think, only twenty-three hours until I have my very own copy of the New Testament in my language!" Their hunger was evident after the dedication as men and women sat down and began intently reading their new copies of God's Word. As I watched, tears streamed down my face. God's Word was shedding light and joy on His people—a people locked for centuries in darkness!

Today, many years later, thousands of Chuj Christians continue to radiate joy as they explore God's Word. In 1999, eight of us in our family had the amazing privilege of returning to Guatemala for the dedication of the whole Chuj Bible.

What is your relationship to God's Word? Does it resemble the insatiable hunger of the Chuj people, or is it like that of the average American Christian? Many people who call themselves Christians rarely, if ever, read the Bible on their own.

Listening to our Heavenly Father by spending time in His Word is the second key to joy. True joy can't be discovered without it. To utilize the other keys to joy, spending time in the Scriptures must be one of our first priorities. Each key is revealed in God's Word. In Jeremiah 15:16, we discover nothing feeds our hungry soul and brings joy to our sorrowing heart more than our Father's precious love letter to us.

In chapter 2, I mentioned my decision to read and study nothing but God's Word for one year and the dramatic change it brought to my life. As I have continued to study His Word the fruit has been a growing, personal joy.

Here are suggestions on how to study His Word. Try each one, and determine which ones are best for you.

Carve Out Time

To read and study God's Word requires giving a part of your day to the Lord. If you are a morning person, get up earlier and start your day with the Lord. Try coffee with Christ or lunch with the Lord; or consider giving some of your TV time to the Lord. Begin with a small commitment—even five minutes a day—and increase it as your hunger grows.

Bible Reading

Regular Bible reading is important, but where do you begin? Try to discover an approach that increases your desire to read the Scriptures. Here are a few ways to read through Bible:

- Using a simple formula, read three chapters a day and five on Sunday. This way you'll read the whole Bible in a year. But remember, the idea for reading the Bible is not to get through it quickly. Make sure you take the time to meditate on what it says.

- Go to our website (www.RRbooks.org) to find a very simple, yet effective way to read through the Bible. You can read in any order you want and take as long as you want. You simply mark off the passages you have read.

- YouVersion.com and BibleGateway.com have many available translations as well as various reading plans. They are available on the computer and on many smart phones and tablets. I (Gaylyn) use YouVersion on my iPad every day. I love how I can quickly go back and forth between translations and I can compare parallel translations.

- Go to your Christian bookstore and find a Bible that has a Bible reading plan in it.

We both like a less-structured approach—reading until we discover a nugget, a "love note" from the Lord. It may be a challenge, a promise, or a command. We stop and chew on it a while before going on, usually thanking Him for this truth. We may also look up other Scriptures that shed light on the discovery.

Memorize God's Word

Several years ago, Colombian terrorists captured our dear friend Chet Bitterman, holding him until they killed him. He had a lifetime commitment to memorize God's Word and had just finished memorizing all of 1 Peter before his kidnapping. To our amazement, joy filled his letters to his wife Brenda, as he quoted verse after verse of Scripture.

What if someone kidnapped you today? Have you memorized any verses to bring joy and comfort? Yes, it's hard work. But it brings great spiritual strength and joy. A guided plan may help. Look online to find something that may help you.

You may want to pick your own verses. Begin with Scriptures that bring you joy. Write each verse or passage on a 3x5 card. Review it several times a day for a few weeks, then once a week. Continue adding verses to your list. See "Ideas for Hiding God's Word in Your Heart" on www.365NamesofGod.com.

For nearly 60 years I've tried to consistently hide God's Word in my heart and He has brought remarkable joy. I've "forgotten" many of the Scriptures, but the Holy Spirit still brings them to mind when I need them. The verses I want to review are on my iPad where I have instant access to them.

Fill Your Mind with Scripture

Whether working at home or driving, it's easy for the mind to wander. To refocus on Christ, ask God to bring a Scripture to mind, and then go over it a few times. To flood your mind with God's Word try praise music, especially Scripture put to music.

Another way of immersing yourself in God's Word is by listening to the Bible on CD or Mp3. It is available in different versions, in either dramatized or simple reading formats.

Meditate on Scripture

Joshua 1:8 says to meditate on God's Word day and night. Here are some ideas on how to do this:

- Choose a verse or any portion of Scripture and reflect on it.

- Substitute your name a situation where appropriate in the verse, and personalize it.

- Consider the meaning of each word.

- Ask the Lord, "Why did you say that? What are you saying to me right now through this?"

- Mull over how it applies to you and how you respond to it.

When you discover a comforting truth such as in Isaiah 40:11, which reads, "He gathers the lambs in his arms and carries them close to his heart," stop and let it soak in. Try to see and feel yourself as a lamb lovingly held in God's strong arms, snuggled close to His warm heart. Let His loving care for you fill you with joy.

Pray Through Scripture

Fellowship with the Lord is a major reason for spending time in His Word. As you read and study, talk with the Author about what He's saying to you and how you should respond to Him.

- When you discover one of God's attributes, praise Him for who He is.

- When the Word convicts you of sin, confess it to Him and repent.

- Use Paul's prayers in Ephesians 1:15-19; 3:14-21; or Colossians 1:9-11 as guidelines to pray for family and friends.

If praying through Scripture is a new concept, begin today by reading Ephesians 1:3-14 and thanking God for each of the nearly twenty spiritual blessings mentioned there.

Get Involved in a Bible Study Group

Being in a study group adds new dimensions to your own study. God will use the experience of others to bring out truths you may have missed and to amplify truths you already know. Try to find at least one other person to study with.

Dig Deeper into Scripture

When my (Gaylyn's) son, Jonathan, was six or seven, he loved to hunt for treasure. When he walked along the beach, his excitement mounted with the possibility of finding a valued prize. What if we approached God's Word with the excitement of a treasure hunt? Countless treasures await discovery in Scripture, but we must dig them out through study and personal application. Here are some ideas for digging deeper:

1. *Ask questions.* As you read the Bible, ask questions like, "What does the passage say?" "What does it mean?" Look up unfamiliar words in a dictionary or Bible dictionary. Then ask, "Why did God say this? What is He saying to me? How can I apply these truths?"

2. *Do a word or subject study.* Choose a topic or idea that interests you. Look up all words relating to it in a concordance, topical reference book, computer Bible program, or online at www.BibleGateway.com. Read each verse in its context. Or try reading or skimming God's Word to look for the topic. Then meditate on your discoveries, recording what you learn and possibly arranging them into a logical outline. I went through the New Testament to discover everything God has done, is doing, and will do for us. These truths bring me great joy!

3. *Do a book or chapter study.* Choose a section, chapter or book of the Bible, and read it several times in different translations. Using different colored pencils, mark repeated words, phrases, and themes. Then summarize each topic, and

personalize an application. Make your own outline of the section, and pick a key verse.

I must admit that I'm not always eager to spend time with God every day. Ups and downs are normal. If your love for the Word isn't as strong as you wish, ask the Lord to cause it to grow, and in His time, He will. God wants us to come to Him and His Word out of loving desire, not because of duty or fear that He'll be angry if we don't.

Love begins with commitment. If you haven't made a commitment to fellowship with the Lord daily in His Word, do it now. As you get into the Scriptures, God will bring an ever-increasing joy into your life.

Opening the Door to Joy

Day 1

1. Read "Discovering the Key."

   a. List any new truths you uncovered.

   b. What will you apply from this section?

2. How did Jeremiah respond to God's Word in Jeremiah 15:16?

   a. What does this mean to you?

   b. What feelings did those words give him?

   c. Do you regularly feast on God's Word? If not, what can you do about it? For example, meditate on it more.

3. Which Scriptures do you meditate on to bring joy, especially in the hard times?

   a. Why (or how) do these verses bring you joy?

b. If you don't have any Scriptures that bring you joy, begin to search for verses as you go through this study. Or ask others what verses bring them joy.

4. Read Nehemiah 8:1-12. After the wall was rebuilt around Jerusalem, what did Ezra do?

Then list the ways the people responded to the Word.

a. What did Nehemiah tell the people in verse 10?

b. What does that mean?

c. Why does God want us to find our strength there?

d. How and why did the people celebrate in verse 12?

e. Why would this cause you to celebrate?

5. How and why were the Scriptures written? 2 Timothy 3:16; 2 Peter 1:20-21

6. Journal: Choose one verse from question 3 to write out, personalize, and meditate on.

    a. Write your thoughts, feelings, and insights.

    b. Thank God for what He's revealing to you from His Word.

Day 2

1. Look at what Psalm 19:7-11 says about the Word—what it's called, how it's described, and what it does for us.

What it's called	How it's described	What it does

    a. What does each name and description mean to you?

b. Explain in a practical way how the Word does these things for you.

2. Besides the descriptions in Psalm 19, how else is the Word described?

Psalm 119:89, 96

Jeremiah 23:29

Romans 1:16

Romans 7:12, 14

a. Which description(s) speak to you today?

b. Why and how do they speak to you?

3. Challenge: List other descriptions of the Bible, with Scriptures.

4. Journal: What did you learn today about God's Word? How will you apply it to your life?

Day 3

1. What does the Bible do for believers?

Psalm 119:9

John 17:17

Ephesians 5:26

2 Timothy 3:16-17

a. Which of these do you need most right now?

b. Why?

2. Challenge: Using Scriptures, list other benefits from the Bible. There are over fifty! Meditate on each, finding joy and thanking God for them.

3. The Bible gives at least ninety-six ways to respond to it. How do these verses say we are to respond to the Word?

    Job 23:12

    Psalm 119:11

    Psalm 119:97

    1 Peter 2:2

    a. Which of these describe your response to the Bible?

    b. Which would you like to develop in your life? How could you do this?

4. Challenge: List other methods to respond to the Word, beginning with Psalm 119.

5. How often are we to spend time in the Scriptures? Deuteronomy 17:19; Acts 17:11

6. Journal: Estimate how much time you spend in God's Word daily or weekly.

Are you satisfied with this amount? If not, what could you eliminate from your schedule to permit more time in it? Write your plan of action.

Day 4

1. Read Deuteronomy 11:18-21.

a. List the actions encouraged from the Word.

b. Beside each, write what it means to you and how you can apply it.

2. Read Ephesians 6:10-17. We're engaged in a spiritual battle, and we must wear the armor of God. What is our only offensive weapon? verse 17

a. What does Hebrews 4:12 add to this?

b. How can you use the Bible as a sword?

3. How did David respond to the Scriptures in Psalm 119:20?

a. What does that mean?

b. How do you respond to the Word?

4. Write out your favorite verse on joy.

Why is this verse special to you?

5. Journal: Why do you spend time in God's Word? Is it out of obligation or delight? Does it bring joy or guilt? Explain.

Day 5

1. Review this study. What will bring you more joy from it?

2. How will spending time in the Word increase your joy?

3. Meditate on and memorize a verse from this lesson that will help you find more joy. Write out the verse below.

   What will you do to make that truth come alive for you?

4. Journal:

   a. Set specific, reachable goals for a time when you will meet the Lord in the Word and what you will begin studying.

   b. Write a prayer of commitment to spend more time reading and studying the Bible daily.

   c. Share your plan of action with a friend who has made a commitment to study the Word and will check on your progress frequently. Together you can share what you discover.

CHAPTER 4

Trust Releases Joy

Discovering the Key

My career in sailing lasted one short afternoon. A friend suggested we take his racing sailboat out for a brisk run in the Pacific Ocean. We had a wonderful time. As he deftly handled the sails, I enjoyed "hiking." In sailing language that means leaning out over the water to balance the boat, trussed up in steel and nylon restraints to keep me from going overboard. But as we neared the dock, a sudden fierce wind turned the boat upside down, and the mast stuck in the mud! I fought to get free from the boat, but in the cold, dark water, I couldn't figure out how to release myself. I was quickly running out of air, and my struggles were futile.

When my lungs were ready to burst, the stark reality of imminent death exploded in my mind. But then I was instantly surprised by joy! Two thoughts flooded my thinking: *So this is how I'm going to die! I always wondered!* And, *I feel overwhelmed with peace and joy because I trust my Lord completely.* Trust freed my joy and chased away fear.

How I thank God for that experience. My trust in Him was tested in a new way that afternoon. The result was a peaceful joy that is very difficult to explain unless you've experienced it firsthand. By the way, I still don't know how it happened, but the restraints fell loose and I bobbed to the surface at what seemed my last second. My friend was terrified, thinking I had drowned. But, I was almost disappointed. I was eager to meet Jesus face to face!

Just as I was locked under the water and away from the air, so we are often locked out of joy because we fail to trust God completely. This chapter's study will look at the link connecting joy and trust, help you to measure your own level of trust, and discover what hinders you from trusting God. You will learn how trusting God can release your joy.

Joe Aldrich said, "Joy is…a deep, settled confidence that a loving Heavenly Father is in control of the details of my life." (Aldrich, 1985). Joy doesn't come magically. It only comes through our relationship with God. First, we must see Him in control of everything, even the details of our lives. Then we must trust Him to do what is best for us. Deep joy will be the result—no matter what happens.

Jerry Bridges, in *Trusting God* (1989), connected joy and trust this way: *God does not ask us to rejoice because we have lost our job, or a loved one has been stricken with cancer, or a child has been born with an incurable birth defect. But He does tell us to rejoice because we believe He is in control of those circumstances and is at work through them for our ultimate good.*

We have a choice about how we will respond to our trials. We can worry, get uptight, and complain, or we can choose to trust God and rejoice in Him. Philippians 4:4 tells us we are to rejoice in the Lord always, not just when we feel like it.

I believe thanksgiving in hard times is a crucial building block of trust. How can we trust God without thanking Him? In *One Thousand Gifts*, Ann Voskamp beautifully ties them together with insights like, "It is thanksgiving that shapes a theology of trust…" "The foremost quality of a trusting disciple is gratefulness." "It's only when you live the prayer of thanksgiving that you live the power of trusting God." "Thanks feeds our trust." And, "There is no joy without trust" (Voskamp, 2011).

Every trial tests our trust. We can measure our trust in our Father in two ways. First, we can consider how well we are claiming Romans 8:28 in our difficult circumstances. Do we really stop and pray, "Lord, I thank You because You will use this for good in my life. I don't know how. I can't see it yet. But I rejoice in You right now because I *choose* to trust you."

The second way we can measure our trust is by the degree of peace we feel as we choose to focus on Him in the midst of our trials. I confess, sometimes I find myself reacting like an old Navy slogan advises: "When in danger or in doubt, run in circles, scream and shout!" You can imagine what happens to my joy when I respond like that!

How do you react to difficult circumstances? Does the door to your joy slam and lock you out when things go wrong, because you focus on the problem rather than the Lord?

I find trusting God in the big struggles easier than in the little frustrations. When emergencies crash into my life, I tend to go to the Lord out of desperation. When I pray to Him, He never fails to bring joyful peace into my life. But I let the little struggles sneak up on me. I try to handle them in my own strength. I don't have to trust God for *everything*, do I? Can't I handle anything on my own?

For twenty years I've had unrelenting prostate cancer that has spread to the bones throughout my body, from my neck to my hips. But I'm constantly amazed at the joy God gives as I've grown in my trust in Him as I thank Him for it daily. Friends smile as I tell them, "I'm celebrating twenty years of cancer!"

What kinds of things sneak in and slam the door to your joy because you forget to put them in the Lord's hands? Do trivial predicaments and frustrations become joy-killers in your life? Or maybe you are facing major struggles, and you need the Lord's faithful power if you are going to unlock the door to joy again.

Whether your joy-killers are big or small, trust is an essential key to the door of joy. Trust is based on the keys we studied in the last two chapters. Trusting Him requires a personal, growing relationship with Him through consistent time in His Word.

I experienced peaceful joy at death's door when the sailboat capsized, and today with cancer. Peace and joy are Siamese twins. One doesn't go anywhere without the other. Isaiah 26:3 shows the way to peace, which results in joy: "You will keep in perfect peace all who trust in you, all whose thoughts are fixed on you!" (NLT).

Turning this verse around may help us understand it better. As we trust in the Lord, our minds will be steadfastly fixed on Him, and His response is to keep us in perfect peace. Where we focus our minds determines whether we'll trust God or not and if we will experience His peace and joy.

Verse 4 continues, "Trust in the LORD forever, for the LORD, the LORD himself, is the Rock eternal." Many times Scripture commands us to trust God. This verse tells us our faith is based on who God is, not on our circumstances.

Has adversity caused joy's door to slam in your face? If so, maybe the key you need is to renew your trust in the eternal Rock. Remind yourself that He is in control and is at work for your good. Begin today to focus your mind and heart on His power, wisdom, and unfailing love. As you do, you'll find that locked doors begin to open, your trust in God will deepen, and a growing joy will flow into your heart.

Opening the Door to Joy

Day 1

1. Read "Discovering the Key."

    a. List any new truths you uncovered.

    b. What will you apply from this section?

2. How do we unlock the door to genuine joy? Psalm 33:21

3. Using a dictionary, define trust. Note: trust, faith and belief have similar meanings in the Bible.

4. What command is in each of these verses?

    Psalm 37:3-5

    Psalm 62:8

    John 14:1

5. To trust God, we must know Him. What qualities of God are foundational for a trusting relationship?

    Psalm 13:5

    Psalm 28:7

    Jeremiah 32:17-19

Nahum 1:7

a. Add these to your list begun in chapter 2, Day 3, question 1.

b. Which qualities help you personally trust God most?

6. Challenge: Add other qualities of God to your list, using Scriptures, if possible.

7. Journal: Evaluate how much you trust God today.

a. In what areas are you finding it hard to trust?

b. Write a prayer committing these areas to Him.

Day 2

1. Trust is especially important during hard times. Read 1 Peter 1:6-8.

a. As we trust God in our trials, what is the result?

b. Have you ever experienced this in a trial? Explain.

2. What are other results of trusting God?

Psalm 28:7

Psalm 32:10

Isaiah 25:9

Matthew 21:22

Romans 5:1

1 John 5:13

3. Challenge: List other results of trusting Jesus.

4. Note a difficult time when you trusted God and He brought joy or you experienced one of the other results you just listed.

5. What are some purposes of trials? (More will be examined in chapter 9.)

   Romans 8:17-18, 28-29

   2 Corinthians 4:16-18

   2 Corinthians 12:7-10

   James 1:2-4

6. How does knowing the purposes of trials help you trust God?

7. Journal: What recent trial has slammed joy's door for you?

a. Prayerfully write what you will begin doing today to trust God more in that situation.

b. List two or three promises you can claim for the trial and how you'll use them. For example, each time the trial comes to mind cast it on the Lord according to 1 Peter 5:7. Remind yourself He truly cares for you.

Day 3

1. Who or what are we to trust in and why?

Psalm 115:9-11

Psalm 119:42

Luke 1:45

John 14:1

2. Who or what are we not to trust?

Psalm 118:8-9

Proverbs 11:28; 28:6

3. When should we trust God? Psalm 56:3-4; 62:8

4. What does Proverbs 3:5-6 tell us to do?

What will result?

5. Note a time you trusted God and experienced His guidance.

6. What do you learn from Hebrews 11:6?

7. Journal: What keeps you from trusting God today?

   What can you do to develop your trust?

Day 4

1. Read Romans 15:13.

   a. What is required for being filled with joy and peace?

   b. As you fulfill this prerequisite, what will be the outcome?

2. Read Isaiah 26:3-4. What two things must be done to experience peace and, ultimately, joy?

   a. How long are we to trust the Lord and why? verse 4

   b. What keeps you from experiencing peace?

3. How are peace, trust, and joy related?

   Is joy possible without trusting God? Explain.

4. Challenge: Do a "subject study" (see chap. 3, "Dig Deeper into Scripture") on trust, faith, and belief.

    a. List what we are to trust in and not trust in and why.

    b. What are the results of each?

    c. What else stands out to you?

5. Journal: Who can be a resource to help you grow in your trust?

    a. What can you do to enlist his/her help?

    b. How will you begin? For example, share a specific trial or internal struggle and ask for prayer to help you trust God in it.

    c. Write out your plan for action.

Day 5

1. Review this study. What will help you develop a deeper trust and joy?

2. How will developing your trust increase your joy?

3. Meditate on and memorize a verse from this lesson that will expand your trust and joy. Write out that verse here.

How can you make that truth come alive for you?

4. Journal: Pick one or two friends who have joy's door locked from struggling to trust God. How can you help renew their trust? For example: Invite them to talk about their pain, then listen with a caring heart. Share how God released your joy through a trial. Let them know you will be praying and trusting God to be faithful in their lives. Pray with them. It can be very faith-boosting to hear someone pray for them.

CHAPTER 5

The Holy Spirit Imparts Joy

Discovering the Key

Within seconds, a few lazy raindrops turned into a gale-force, tornado-like wind, lashing out against everything in its path.

My son Timothy and I (Gaylyn) stared in fascination as the angry wind whipped the pounding rain and hail every which way. It pummeled the restaurant windows where we were eating, blinding us to our car ten yards away. "That was close. I'm so glad we didn't get here thirty seconds later," I observed. We watched the water quickly form a small lake *inside* the restaurant, despite its closed door.

As we drove home less than an hour later, the wind and rain had stopped, but the main highway to our house was closed. Why? It was covered with hail and an SUV was stuck in it. Did I mention this was July. Colorado weather can be unpredictable, but that was crazy.

When we got home, three inches of hail covered our lawn. The next day, I assessed the damage: trees and plants stripped of leaves, branches broken, and houses plastered with leaves. My roof and fence were pockmarked and the paint on my house looked like it was sandblasted—or rather rock-blasted.

My insurance adjuster arrived the day after the storm. After she got off my roof she informed me, "We'll pay for a complete paint job for the house, a new, upgraded roof, and stain for your fence and deck." My eyes filled with tears of joy. I needed new paint and stain and a new roof, but didn't have the money to pay for it. But even more amazing—my next door neighbors had no damage to their paint or roof. And their house is less than ten feet from mine! It seems God targeted my house with the fury of the storm, just to bless me, to provide in a very unusual way.

After the adjuster left, I went to the Jericho Center, a house of prayer. That day, I alternated between crying and laughing, because God is so incredibly good. I'm sure people wondered about me. I didn't care. Joy overwhelmed me.

Over the years, God had told me repeatedly that He would take care of me, that He was my provider. And He had always done just that, although just before that storm my income had been very low. I just never expected Him to use the ferocity of rain and hail to meet my needs.

Throughout the day, I thanked and praised the Lord for the unexpected blessing of the storm. In the days preceding the storm, I was meditating on the Hebrew word for spirit, *ruah*, which means wind. By the way, the word *pneuma* in the New Testament also means spirit, wind or breath. Often when I'm walking the trails near my house, viewing Pikes Peak, the gentle breezes and the sudden gusts remind me of the Holy Spirit. Sometimes He brings cool refreshment, at other times a warning to retreat to my home quickly.

That day, I praised the Holy Spirit as I meditated on some of His names from the Word. He is the Spirit of Grace (Heb. 10:29); the Spirit of Wisdom and Revelation, so we'll know Him more (Eph. 1:17); and the Spirit of Life (Rom. 8:2). I've discovered over fifty different names of the Spirit in the Bible. It's amazing to meditate on them. The more I focused on all the Holy Spirit is, the more my spirit overflowed with joy. I kept telling the Lord "thank You, thank You, thank You. You are so good to me."

Often we view the storms in our lives as "bad" It's easy to assume they are God's punishment or that God is not taking care of us. I wonder how often we go through a difficult situation and just look at its destruction and not at God's grace and goodness. How often does the Holy Spirit bring a seeming tornado into our lives to bless us, to bring us joy? How often have we missed the blessings in the storms of our lives? Are we so focused on the hail, rain and damage they bring that we don't take the time to look for God's blessings in them?

I find indescribable joy when I choose to praise the Lord during the storms of my life—even when they threaten to destroy me and I can't see any good that could possibly come from them. However, when I choose to focus on the damage, rather than on God, I can quickly become discouraged.

Are you in the middle of a storm right now? Does it seem like it might destroy you, because the winds are so strong? Take some time to ask the Lord to show you where He is in your situation. Ask Him to show you what blessings He has for you in it. As you learn to see the Holy Spirit's work in the storms of life, you, too, will discover amazing joy.

Over the years, I've sought to know God better so I could worship and praise

Him more. In my search, I began a list of names and qualities of the Lord. My daily prayer became, "Lord, I want to know you more." God loves answering prayers like that. The Lord says that if we seek Him we will find Him (Deut. 4:29; Matt. 7:7-8).

As I read and studied the Word, He began to show me more of Himself. Today I have over 2300 names of the Lord from the Bible. I never in my wildest dreams could have imagined that God had so many different names. *

The unanticipated part of my study of God's names was getting to know the Holy Spirit in new ways, as a personal God. I always had a good relationship with Father God and with Jesus, but I didn't see that I could have an intimate relationship with the Holy Spirit. To me He was more nebulous, less personal than the Father and Jesus. Getting to know Him has brought me so much joy. If you have had the same view of the Spirit, I want to encourage you to spend time getting to know Him. Ask Him to reveal more of Himself to you.

As I have grown in my intimacy with the Holy Spirit, He has released joy in me as I see Him working in and through me. When I see His power at work through my life, sometimes I will start laughing, because God is so good. For example, one evening I was with a friend who had major problems with her spine, which caused pain in her hips, back, neck and head. She'd had the same issues for over sixty years. When I laid hands on her and prayed, the pain immediately went away. She said she could feel heat all up and down her spine. Two days after I prayed for her, she told me the Lord threw in a bonus that I hadn't requested. She was also healed of her severe gluten intolerance. Isn't that just like God to do immeasurably more than we can ask or imagine (Eph. 3:20)? God loves to outdo Himself!

What is your relationship with the Holy Spirit? Does He bring you joy? As you study this chapter and get to know the Him better, I pray you will be filled with an amazing joy.

* I recently wrote a devotional, The Surprising Joy of Exploring God's Heart: A Daily Adventure with 365 of His Names. You can learn more at www. 365NamesofGod. com.

Opening the Door to Joy

Day 1

1. Read "Discovering the Key."

   a. List any new truths you uncovered.

   b. What will you choose to apply from this section?

2. Read Galatians 5:22-23.

   a. What is the connection between the Holy Spirit and joy?

   b. Is this fruit automatic when you have the Spirit in you? Why or why not?

   c. Give an example to illustrate your answer to the previous question.

   d. How do we get the fruit of the Spirit? Do we have to work to produce it or does the Holy Spirit produce it when we are in connection with Him? Explain.

   e. How does John 15:1-8 add to your understanding of fruit? What does it say we need to do to produce fruit?

f. If you don't have all the qualities in Galatians 5:22-23, ask the Holy Spirit to reveal why you don't have them and what you need to do. Then listen and do what He tells you.

3. If you feel like you don't know the Holy Spirit as well as you would like, it's not too late. What do the following verses say to you about seeking God?

   Deuteronomy 4:29

   Jeremiah 29:13

   Matthew 7:7-8 (See also Luke 11:9-10)

4. Challenge: Each of the persons of the Godhead are distinct and you can know each separately. Read the following verses. What do they say to you?

   Psalm 139:7-12

   Isaiah 11:2

   John 14:17

   1 Corinthians 3:3

   Ephesians 1:13-14

   Ephesians 3:14-19

   Hebrews 10:29

2 Timothy 1:7

5. Journal: How well do you know the Holy Spirit? Write a prayer, asking the Spirit to reveal more of Himself to you through this study and through your continued study of Him.

Day 2

1. Read Luke 10:17-21 (start at verse one to see the whole story).

   a. How does verse 17 say the disciples reacted when they shared with Jesus about their ministry?

   b. What does verse 21 say about where Jesus found His joy?

   c. How much joy did Jesus have? What do you think that might have looked like?

   d. Why was Jesus full of joy? See verses 17-20.

   e. What was Jesus' response to the joy He received from the Holy Spirit in verse 21?

   f. Have you ever experienced the full joy that Jesus had from the Holy Spirit? Why or why not? If you're not sure, take some time to talk to the Lord about it.

   g. How can you imitate Jesus from these verses?

2. Read Isaiah 61:1-3. In Luke 4:17-19, Jesus quoted part of this passage, saying He fulfilled it that day.

   a. What four things does verse 3 say the Spirit anoints us to do?

   b. Gladness is used in some translations and is another word for joy. What is your response to God offering you joy in place of your mourning?

   c. Read Isaiah 61:1-3 again as your declaration today. Say something like, "I declare that the Spirit of the Lord God is on me, because the Lord has anointed me..." Making declarations about what is true is a powerful way to change your thoughts and your life. Did you know what you say about and to yourself has a greater effect on you than anything anybody else says about you?

3. Journal: Jesus relied on the Holy Spirit in every way. He showed us how we, too, can have a relationship with the Holy Spirit. Look at some or all of the following passages and write down what Jesus' relationship was with the Holy Spirit and how you can imitate Him.

   Matthew 10:10

   Matthew 12:28 (see verses 22-28)

   Mark 13:11

   Luke 4:1, 14

   Luke 4:18-19

   John 3:34

   John 6:63

4. Challenge: Look up the following verses and meditate on them. Write down what you learn about the Holy Spirit through them.

Romans 8:14

Romans 8:26-27

Ephesians 5:18-20

2 Thessalonians 2:13

Day 3

1. Read Acts 13:49-52.

a. What happened in verse 50?

b. The disciples could have been angry, discouraged or any number of other responses. What was their reaction in verse 52?

c. What two things filled them after they were persecuted and expelled from the region?

d. Ask the Lord to show you the connection between being filled with joy and with the Holy Spirit. Write down what He shows you.

e. Have you ever experienced anything like that? When? Explain.

f. What can you apply to your life from this scenario?

2. Read Philippians 1:17-20.

   a. What was happening to Paul in verse 17? Notice where he was.

   b. Why was Paul rejoicing?

   c. What can you learn from Paul's example?

3. Read 1 Thessalonians 1:6.

   a. What was happening with the Thessalonians?

   b. What is the connection here between joy and the Holy Spirit?

4. Read Romans 5:3-5.

   a. What is the relationship between the Holy Spirit and joy?

   b. What can you apply from these verses to your life now?

5. At the beginning of the chapter, I shared about seeing the Holy Spirit in the wind. Read Luke 8:22-25. It uses the same Greek word for wind as is used for the Spirit, *pneuma*.

   a. What was Jesus doing during the storm?

   b. What did He do when the disciples woke Him?

    c. Are you in a storm right now? If so, do you need to ask Jesus to calm it, or do you need to speak to the storm yourself like Jesus did in Mark 4:35-41?

6. Journal: Ask the Lord to show you how the Holy Spirit is like the wind. How have you experienced Him as a wind?

Day 4

1. Read Romans 14:17.

    a. What three things does this verse say about the Kingdom of God?

    b. What is the relationship between the Holy Spirit and joy?

    c. What might you need to do to apply that connection to your life?

2. Look at the following verses. What is the link between the Holy Spirit and joy? How might the Holy Spirit bring you joy through them?

    Romans 15:13

    1 Thessalonians 5:16-19

3. We're going to look at what Jesus said about the Holy Spirit and joy in John 14-16.

   a. What did Jesus say He would ask the Father in John 14:16?

   b. What are the Holy Spirit's names in 14:16?

   c. What does 14:25 say the Holy Spirit will do?

   d. In 16:7, what does Jesus say will happen when He left them?

   e. In 16:15, what will the Holy Spirit do?

   f. In 16:19-20, how did Jesus say the disciples would feel at first when He left them?

   g. In verse 20, Jesus says that their grief would turn to joy. Why would it turn to joy? What had Jesus just been talking about earlier in this chapter?

4. Challenge: Read John 14 through 16 to see what else you can learn about the Holy Spirit and joy. Write what you discover.

5. Journal: How has the Holy Spirit brought you joy? When have you seen the joy He's brought?

Day 5

1. Review this study. What will help you to allow the Holy Spirit to release His joy in you?

2. What holds you back from having a deeper relationship with the Holy Spirit?

3. Meditate on and memorize a verse from this lesson that will help you find more joy. Write the verse below.

   How can you make this truth come alive for you?

4. What has stood out to you the most from this chapter?

5. Journal: Write a prayer of commitment to follow through on what you learned in this study. Record any new insights the Lord gave you.

CHAPTER 6

Obedience Restores Joy

Discovering the Key

As a Christian counselor, I have learned much about life through my clients. One truth confronts me all too frequently—obey God and have joy; disobey Him and be miserable. How could anything be simpler, yet so often missed?

Brad and Jean were a Christian couple. Both had excellent jobs. Both were successful by the world's standards. It seemed like they had it all, but they were miserable. After a short time, each new toy they bought or each new pleasure pursued left a bitter taste. They sought desperately for a morsel of joy everywhere they went, but could find none.

Finally they came to me for help. Maybe counseling could rekindle their joy. In a short time, we discovered neither Brad nor Jean had taken the Lord or His Word very seriously since they came to know Him. As we looked more closely at their lives, we found a telltale pile of "little" sins that had been kept from the sight of others. They spent nearly every penny they earned, yet they felt they could only afford to give God a dollar or two each week. Then there were the ungodly movies, music and the Web sites they sought out, the little lies they told each other, and the missed opportunities to share Christ. The list went on and on.

They came to me thinking that counselors have a magic wand for joy. If I would only wave it over them, joy would appear, with little effort on their part. Unfortunately, joy isn't magic.

As the weeks went by, Brad and Jean began to discover the answers to their unhappiness. They were free to choose. But those choices had a price. For them, the cost meant abandoning their sinful life-style and working toward a right relationship with the Lord. Simple obedience to God's commands was the missing key to their joy.

I wish I could say this story had a happy ending—it doesn't. After a few weeks of thinking about it, they decided the cost was too high. Sin was more fun than joy, and that's what they wanted. Misery could be tolerated, but full commitment to the Lord looked too difficult, too frightening, too costly. They later divorced.

It's true; joy has its price—obedience. But that price isn't too costly. God says His commands are "not burdensome" (1 John 5:3). Pleasing our Heavenly Father brings profound joy. Jesus put it this way in Luke 11:28: "Blessed rather are those who hear the word of God and obey it." If you want joy—get God's blessing. If you want His blessing—obey His Word. It's that easy—and that difficult.

God doesn't sell joy. He gives it away—to those who love Him. And those who love Him demonstrate their love by obeying His commands (John 14:15, 21, 24; 1 John 5:3). The psalmist said, "Light shines on the righteous and joy on the upright in heart" (Psalm 97:11).

John Piper, in *Desiring God*, (2003) says we lose our joy through disobedience. "Sin is like spiritual leprosy. It deadens your spiritual senses so that you rip your soul to shreds and don't even feel it." If you're struggling to find more joy, examine your soul to see if you have any little rips in it. In some area of your life, are you consistently not doing what God wants? Like sugar trickling out of a torn bag, joy leaks out of those rips.

If we're deliberately disobeying His Word, how can we expect God to give us His full measure of joy? We can't take a partial measure—obey just a little and therefore get a little joy.

Scripture specifically tells us that obedience reaps a bountiful harvest. Recently, I read every Bible verse on obeying God. I discovered thirty-two wonderful promises to those who obey Him. These promises guaranteed to bring joy to the heart. If we are obedient, we are promised to receive answers to prayer and enjoy long life. It will also go well with us and our children, and God will richly bless us and keep His covenant of love with us. The blessings for obedience are limitless. We'll consider more of them in our study section.

While we see that obeying our Lord brings great joy, it also presents a subtle danger for us. Our motivation for obeying Him must not be merely to get joy—then we'd be trying to buy joy from Him. We obey Him because we love Him, not for what He will do for us. Jesus made this clear, "Anyone who loves me will obey my teaching. . . . Anyone who does not love me will not obey my teaching" (John 14:23-24). We also obey because we desire an intimate relationship with Jesus as our friend (John 15:14).

If you have been consistently disobedient or if your motives for obedience have been wrong, you may be feeling guilty. But be encouraged—God doesn't expect us to live in sinless perfection. Everyone falls at times. God knows we'll fall, so He sent

His Son to die on the cross to pay for our sins. He only expects a commitment to walk in the light, obeying Him as well as we can, through His strength. He then covers our failures and shows us the right way to live.

The apostle John, inspired by the Spirit, put it this way, "But if we walk in the light, as he is in the light, we have fellowship with one another, and the blood of Jesus, his Son, purifies us from all sin" (1 John 1:7). The Greek text clearly shows that His blood *continually* purifies us from every sin. Keep on walking in the light, and when you fall, Jesus will reach down and gently pick you up. Verse 9 tells us when we do sin, we must confess it, and then God will forgive us and purify us.

Obedience is the outward expression of a heart that has turned to God (Psalm 119:65-68, 72). Obedience and joy cling together like a teenage boy and girl in love.

This fifth key, obedience, is extremely important in opening the door to joy. We urge you to ask God to reveal any sins in your life that might be a barrier to your joy. Confess these to the Lord, and determine in His strength to begin obeying Him in those areas. As you obey, your joy will be restored and will increase.

Opening the Door to Joy

Day 1

1. Read "Discovering the Key."

    a. List any new truths you uncovered.

    b. What will you choose to apply from this section?

2. Read John 15:9-13. What does verse 9 tell us to do? Why?

    a. What does that mean to you?

    b. How does verse 10 tell us to remain in Jesus' love?

    c. What is Jesus' command in verse 12?

    d. How is He our example?

3. What is one result of obedience? John 15:11

    a. Is it worth it? Why or why not?

    b. Whose joy did Jesus want us to have? Describe His joy.

4. Joy is one result of obeying God. What are other results God promised?

    Deuteronomy 28:2

    Joshua 1:7

    Job 36:11

    Psalm 19:100

    1 John 2:5

    1 John 3:22-24

5. What should characterize our obedience? Joshua 1:7; Psalm 40:8

6. Challenge: List other results of obedience. Begin with 1 Kings 3:14 and Nehemiah 1:5.

    Which motivate you the most? Why?

7. What happens when you disobey God?

    Jeremiah 11:3

    Jeremiah 32:23

    Ezekiel 20:13

Hosea 9:1

8. Challenge: Read the Book of Jonah. What principles do you learn from Jonah's experience?

Which ones can you apply?

9. Journal: Meditate on John 15:9-13.

   a. In verse 11, how much joy does Jesus want us to have?

   b. How often do you experience this kind of joy? Explain.

   c. How can you experience it more often?

Day 2

1. What do Leviticus 18:4; Joshua 22:5; and Jeremiah 7:23 command?

2. How are we told to obey?

   Deuteronomy 11:13-14

   Psalm 119:5, 34

   Zechariah 6:15

   Ephesians 6:5-6

    a. Evaluate and describe your own obedience in light of these verses.

    b. If you don't have this type of obedience, what could you do about it?

3. How long and often are we to obey God? Psalm 119:44; 2 Corinthians 2:9

4. What are some ways we can obey God?

    Micah 6:8

    2 Corinthians 10:5

    1 Peter 1:14-16

5. Who and what are we to obey?

    Joshua 24:24

    Ephesians 6:1, 5

    Titus 3:1

    1 Peter 1:22

    1 Peter 3:6

    2 John 1:6

    a. Which is the most difficult for you to obey? Why?

    b. If we must choose, whom does Acts 4:19 and 5:29 say we must obey?

6. Challenge: Read Nehemiah 1:5, John 14:15-24, and 1 John 5:3.

    a. What is the relationship between loving and obeying God?

    b. What do we know about the person who obeys God?

7. Journal: What is God saying to you today about obeying Him? Honestly look at your life and write what God shows you.

    Then ask His forgiveness for those areas of disobedience and His help to overcome them.

Day 3

1. Jesus is our supreme example of obedience.

    a. What can we learn about Jesus' obedience from:

    Luke 2:51

    Romans 5:19

    Hebrews 12:2

    b. Meditate on these verses and list ways Jesus was obedient.

2. Read Mark 14:32-36, 39. Briefly describe the scene.

a. How was Jesus feeling? verses 33-34

b. What did He pray three times? Of what cup did He speak?

c. How did Jesus show His obedience to the Father in these verses?

3. What does Hebrews 5:7-9 say about Jesus and His submission to the Father?

a. Define submission and obedience, or look them up in a dictionary.

b. How are submission and obedience similar? How are they different?

4. Read and meditate on Philippians 2:5-11.

a. What do you learn about Jesus?

b. Write a note thanking Jesus for suffering this for you.

5. How did Jesus view His relationship with God? See John 4:34.

6. Journal: From studying Jesus' life today, what principles for obedience can you draw for your life?

Specifically how will you apply these?

Day 4

1. How did David respond to God's Word in Psalm 119:14?

   a. What did he compare it to?

   b. How eager are you to obey God's Word? Explain.

2. Challenge: Read Genesis 12:1-4, 17:19, and 22:1-23. If you have time, read chapters 12-22.

   a. What were two of Abraham's acts of obedience?

   b. List principles from Abraham's life that you can apply to your life.

3. Those who obey are often called righteous or upright.

   a. What do you learn from Psalm 97:11 and 118:15?

   b. What does this say to you about how you can experience more joy?

4. Read Jeremiah 11:7-8 and 22:21. What did God say to the Israelites?

   a. Could He say this about you?

   b. How did they respond and what was the result?

    c. How do you respond to God's warnings?

    d. If needed, write a prayer asking God to forgive you and help you change.

5. What are we to turn away from, and what are we to obey? Romans 6:12-17

6. Is neglecting a command just as wrong as disobeying a command? Explain.

    a. How did Saul neglect a command? 1 Samuel 15

    b. What resulted?

7. Journal: What have you neglected doing that you know God wants done?

    Confess it, ask God for the strength to obey, then write specifically how you will obey.

Day 5

1. Review this study on obedience. How has God spoken to you specifically this week?

2. What can you get from this study that will bring you more joy?

3. Give an example of when an act of obedience restored your joy.

4. List each key we've studied in previous chapters.

   a. How are you applying them?

   b. How is God using them to open your door to joy?

5. Meditate on and memorize a verse from this lesson that will help you find more joy. Write out this verse below.

   What will you do to make that truth spring to life for you?

6. Journal: Prayerfully consider and list any areas where you're not being completely obedient.

   a. What is God saying to you today about these?

   b. Ask Him to help you obey Him.

CHAPTER 7

Prayer Maintains Joy

Discovering the Key

When I reflect over years past, I see peaks in my joy. It's similar to the time I viewed snow-capped mountain summits pushing through the clouds while flying over the Andes in South America. In my own life, I'm surprised how many of these joy peaks rose from prayer.

Some of those prayers came out of desperation. One time in Guatemala, when we were living in a remote mountain village, my wife Bobble hovered close to death with hepatitis. It was impossible to move her or for anyone to come to help her. Finally, after six agonizing weeks, she seemed strong enough to make the long, exhausting trip over treacherous dirt roads to a hospital.

A pounding rain drenched the mountains all night before our trip. At four a.m., we tucked little 2-year old Gaylyn and year-old Joy into the back of our Jeep, along with three Chuj friends—a seventy-year-old man dying of tuberculosis, a fourteen-year-old girl to help care for our daughters, and an eleven-year-old boy, Caxin (pronounced "Cash-een"), who was helping us learn the Chuj language.

We soon discovered the trip would be even more dangerous than we thought. Negotiating the steep horse trail that served as our road was a nightmare. That day the words *mud*, *mire*, *muck*, *slither*, and *slide* took on new meanings.

Six grueling hours passed—then disaster. While going up a particularly steep mountain, the Jeep began a sickening slide backwards and wedged itself into the mountainside. Two and a half agonizing hours passed while we tried everything, but the Jeep wouldn't budge. I began to panic. After eight and a half hours, we had only covered seven miles through that wilderness, and the nearest place to spend the night was still fifty-three grueling miles away. Bobble could die on that desolate, ten-thousand-foot mountain.

As we considered our hopeless situation, Caxin said, "Do you think we could pray and ask God to help us?" My first thought was, *I'm the missionary. Why didn't I think of that?* So we all stood in a little circle and cried out to the Lord.

As soon as we stopped praying, Caxin noticed some long poles in the brush. We were able to pry the back wheels up out of the mud and push big rocks underneath them. The Jeep drove right out. After only ten minutes, we were on our way again! It took over twelve hours to cover sixty miles to the nearest town where we could stay overnight. The next day we drove ten more hours to reach the hospital. But can you imagine our joy at seeing God work in that "impossible" situation?

Today, many years later, joy floods my heart again when I remember how our powerful Lord protected us and kept Bobble alive through prayer. And I rejoice that through this experience He taught me a lifelong lesson. Before that time, my normal response to a crisis was panic, and if all else failed, I would try prayer. Now, my goal is to respond with prayer first.

What's your usual response to a crisis? Do you panic and only use prayer as a last resort? Or do you "cast your cares on the Lord" as He teaches us in Psalm 55:22? (Also see 1 Peter 5:7.) It's pretty obvious which response will bring joy. Jesus pointed out that answered prayer fills us with joy when He said in John 16:24, "Ask and you will receive, and your joy will be complete."

Some of my greatest joy comes through praying for others. As I looked up all the biblical references to prayer, I was amazed to discover nearly 90 percent were about praying for others rather than for ourselves.

Are you as delighted when God answers your prayers for other people as when He answers prayer for you? This attitude is one sign of a healthy prayer life. Another sign of a healthy prayer life is praying through the prayers in God's Word.

When our three daughters were teen-agers, Bobbie and I searched for ways to help them through those wonderful, frightening years. We worked hard at loving them and tried to be effective parents. The Lord showed me that being a good parent wasn't enough. My daughters were engaged in all-out warfare with the enemy of their souls. Nothing less than a deliberate, fervent, and persistent prayerful assault on him and his evil kingdom was needed.

Colossians 1:9-11 served as a model prayer for them. I memorized it, and determined by God's grace to pray through these verses every day for each of my daughters. Throughout those teen years, the Father heard this daily prayer, "Lord, please fill _____ with the knowledge of Your will through all spiritual wisdom and understanding, that she may live a life worthy of You and may please You in every good work, growing in the knowledge of You, being strengthened with all power according to Your glorious might so that she may have great endurance and patience and may joyfully give You thanks." Can you imagine a more relevant prayer for a teenager in today's world? When you pray God's Word, you gain the added benefit of confidence that you're praying God's will.

We had our share of struggles during those years. Praying that prayer didn't magically deliver us from hard times, but it did bring joy in the midst of them. Today, joy fills our hearts as we see how the Lord has answered that prayer in each of our daughters' lives.

Make praying for the important people in your life a priority. One way to do this effectively is to pray one of Paul's prayers for them, such as Philippians 1:9-11 or Ephesians 3:16-19.

If you want greater joy, focus on your prayer life. Learn to turn to God in prayer first in every situation. As you do, you'll lay a foundation for years of joy ahead.

Opening the Door to Joy

Day 1

1. Read "Discovering the Key."

    a. List any new truths you uncovered.

    b. What will you apply from this section?

2. What does John 16:22-24 tell us to do?

    What are the two results?

3. What does Philippians 4:6-7 tell us to do, not to do, and the result?

4. List more results of prayer from Job 33:26.

5. Which results have you experienced from questions 2-4? Explain.

    What keeps you from benefitting from the others?

6. What does God promise in these verses, and what is our responsibility?

Isaiah 41:17

Jeremiah 33:3

1 John 3:21-23

a. Which promise can you hold onto today?

b. How can you experience it?

7. Read Genesis 24:45 and Daniel 9:20-23.

a. When did God answer the prayers?

b. Have you ever experienced a similar response to prayer? Explain.

8. Challenge: What do you learn about prayer from Acts 12:1-17 and 16:22-34? Also, read or skim through the whole book of Acts and list the principles of prayer you glean.

9. Share a time you experienced an answer to prayer.

If you haven't experienced any answers, what might be the reason?

10. What is God's promise to us in Isaiah 56:7?

11. Journal: Write about a time you experienced joy in prayer.

Day 2

1. What three things does Colossians 4:2 command us to do?

2. Read 1 Timothy 2:1-4.

    a. List and define the types of prayer mentioned.

    b. Who are we to pray for and why?

3. Who should pray to God? Psalm 32:6; Proverbs 15:8

4. How are we to come to God and why? Hebrews 4:14-16; 10:19-23

5. How often should we pray? Acts 10:2; 1 Thessalonians 5:17

6. Why are we to pray? 2 Thessalonians 1:12

7. How are we to pray for others?

    Philippians 1:4

    Colossians 4:12

    1 Thessalonians 3:10

8. What action accompanied prayer in Ezra 8:23; Daniel 9:3; and Acts 13:3?

    a. How does Matthew 6:17-18 say to fast and not to fast?

    b. What will result?

9. Challenge: Study fasting beginning in 2 Samuel 12:13-23; Isaiah 58:3-9; Zechariah 8:19; and Luke 2:37. Record what you learn.

10. Journal: Honestly evaluate your prayer life. What areas from today's study do you need more work on?

    Write a specific plan and a prayer of commitment to spend more time in prayer.

Day 3

1. When did Jesus, our teacher and example in prayer, pray? Mark 1:35

    When do you take time to pray?

2. Where did He pray? Matthew 14:23

    Where do you meet the Lord to pray? 3. Read Matthew 6:5-8. What did Jesus teach about prayer?

    a. How should we not pray?

b. Where should we pray and how?

c. What will result?

d. What does God know already? verse 8

4. What principles can you learn for your prayer life from Matthew 6:9-15?

   How will you apply them today?

5. What else did Jesus want to teach His disciples in Luke 18:1?

   a. Do you ever feel like giving up? If so, when?

   b. What would help you? See Psalm 55:22.

6. Challenge: What do you learn about prayer from Luke 18:1-8?

7. Read Matthew 26:36-45. Just before His arrest, how was Jesus feeling?

   a. What did He pray three times?

   b. Whose will did He want?

   c. What did Jesus tell the disciples to do and why? verse 41

   d. Describe a time your spirit was willing, but your body weak.

e. What could have helped you?

8. Journal: What will you apply today from Jesus' example and teachings about prayer? Write out how you will apply it.

Day 4

1. What do you learn about prayer from James 5:13-18?

   a. What does verse 17 say about Elijah?

   b. How can you follow Elijah's example?

2. How is Epaphras described in Colossians 4:12?

   Could this be said of you? Why or why not?

3. What did Paul pray for others? As you read each passage, personalize it for someone you know. Use these verses regularly to pray for others.

   Ephesians 1:15-19

   Ephesians 3:14-21

4. How do each of these prayers begin? What do you learn about God?

1 Kings 8:23

2 Kings 19:15

Jeremiah 32:17

Acts 4:24

5. Where should our focus be when we begin to pray?

Where is your focus when you pray? On you, your problems or on God?

6. How did God answer these prayers? Write a principle for prayer gleaned from each passage.

1 Samuel 1:27 (See verses 10-27)

1 Kings 18:36-38 (See verses 16-39)

2 Kings 6:17-18, 20 (See verses 8-23)

Acts 9:40-41 (See verses 36-42)

7. Challenge: Read 2 Chronicles 20:1-30 and/or Nehemiah 1:1-2:9.

a. Write the problem and responses.

b. List the steps used in the prayer and the results.

c. What can you apply from these verses to improve your prayer life?

8. Journal: Read Luke 1:37.

a. What in your life looks impossible right now?

b. Write Jeremiah 32:17 as your prayer.

c. What is your response to these verses?

Day 5

1. Review this study on prayer. In what ways can prayer help unlock your joy?

2. Explain how prayer maintains joy, and give a personal example.

3. Meditate on and memorize a verse from this lesson that will help you find more joy. Write out the verse below.

How will you make that truth spring to life for you?

4. Journal: If you don't have a prayer journal, get a notebook and begin listing requests for yourself and others. When a prayer is answered, record it and rejoice over it. Begin your prayer list by writing down the names of at least five people and praying for each one. It is very faith-boosting to look back at all the answers to prayer.

CHAPTER 8

Worship Unleashes Joy

Discovering the Key

I ran to my car and took off for school on the last day of the semester. I was eager to be on time to turn in my two term papers due that day. I didn't mind the two-hour drive from Orange County to graduate school in San Diego. It was a quiet time to think, pray, and review Scripture. But today, forty-five minutes after leaving home, it dawned on me that I had forgotten my term papers. Frustration and anger engulfed me as I thought about going all the way back to get them. To make matters worse, there was no place to turn around on the freeway.

As I drove ahead fuming until I could turn around, a verse of Scripture pushed through the hard, dry ground of my frustration and blossomed in my mind. Have you ever learned a verse, then really wished you hadn't? The Lord has a way of driving those piercing truths into our minds just when we want them the least, but need them the most. In this instance it was Ephesians 5:20, "Always giving thanks to God the Father for everything in the name of our Lord Jesus Christ."

My immediate reaction was, "No way. Lord. The last thing I feel right now is thankful." The Lord gently reminded me, "I didn't say, 'feeling thankful.' I said, 'giving thanks.' There's a difference." "OK, Lord," I said, "You win. Thanks for saving me. Thanks for my wife. Thanks for my three girls. I really don't feel like doing this, Lord. Isn't that enough?" The Lord replied, "'Always,' and 'for everything.'"

I faced a choice to obey or not. I could give thanks, no matter how I felt. Or I could be miserable. So I chose to begin thanking Him for everything I could think of. By the time I turned around and started back home, the frustration and anger started to retreat.

I thanked God in new ways that day and for things I had never thought of thanking Him for before. I thanked Him for a healthy liver. Spleen. Lungs. Heart. Bones. Brain. Toes. It turned into a full-blown worship time, as grateful praise welled in me. By the time I got back home, ninety minutes after I left, joy was gushing out of my heart. With concern, my wife Bobbie asked, "What are you doing back home?" With a huge smile, I joyfully burst out, "I forgot my term papers!" I had some explaining to do as I picked Bobbie off the floor.

Looking back, that day was one of the best of my life. The incredible joy I experienced in worshiping the Lord for so long was part of it. But even more, I learned a lesson I will never forget—my emotions don't have to be dominated by circumstances. When things go wrong it's normal to feel bad. But I can trade those feelings for joy, *if* I choose to worship my Lord through grateful praise and thanksgiving. And you can do the same.

Worship has a special relationship to joy. It is both a key to joy and an expression of joy. Are you down? You can worship God and experience true joy. Are you truly joyful? If so, you will express it best through worship. Grateful worship and joy are inseparable.

First Thessalonians 5:18 is often quoted alone: "Give thanks in all circumstances, for this is God's will for you in Christ Jesus." It's a wonderful verse, but it shouldn't be quoted without verses 16 and 17, because the three verses are one sentence. It begins, "Rejoice always; pray continually." The Greek is clear that all three parts together make up God's will for us.

The word used in "pray continually" doesn't mean merely asking for things. Rather, it expresses devotion and includes worship, praise, and thanksgiving. So if you want to be joyful always, you must also worship God and give Him thanks always. If you want to be in God's will, obey these three commands—not just when everything is going fine, but all the time.

When your joy seems like the Titanic heading out to sea, don't strain your spiritual muscles to try to pull it back in your own strength. Try grateful worship instead. Get your mind off yourself, and begin to worship your wonderful Lord. Praise Him for who He is, and thank Him for everything. I dare you to do this and remain miserable.

God provides many examples in His Word of His people responding to bad times with worship and praise. Second Chronicles 20 is my favorite example. A huge army was on the march to obliterate Judah. Their leader Jehoshaphat was terrified, but he called everyone together to pray. He began by worshipping God for who He is and what He had done for them.

At the end of his beautiful prayer he confessed, "We have no power to face this vast army that is attacking us. We do not know what to do, but our eyes are on you" (verse 12). The Lord responded with words of encouragement, but they still had to face the overwhelming army.

Then Jehoshaphat and all Judah did something outrageous. They worshiped and praised the Lord. As if that weren't enough, he appointed a choir to sing praises to the Lord. Do you know where the choir performed? Out in front of Judah's army as they marched into battle! Imagine volunteering for that choir!

Then the most amazing thing happened as they began to sing and praise. God took up the battle for them and utterly defeated the attacking forces. The enemy even helped kill each other until not one man was left alive. Afterwards, they praised the Lord for what He had done and even renamed the place "Valley of Praise."

I was challenged to discover what they praised God for when they were still in deep trouble. They praised Him for the splendor of His holiness. When you can see nothing in your circumstances to be thankful for, you can always focus on the Lord and praise Him for who He is. When you do, you can be sure He'll be very close.

God's people repeatedly had the same response to suffering as Jehoshaphat. David often responded with praise. In Psalm 69:29-30 he said "But as for me, afflicted and in pain—may your salvation, God, protect me. I will praise God's name in song and glorify him with thanksgiving." Bound in stocks in a dark dungeon, after being stripped and beaten severely, Paul and Silas also prayed and praised God in song (Acts 16:22-25). Even Stephen focused on the Lord while being stoned to death by a crazed mob (Acts 7:54-60).

When everything seems to go wrong, and you feel your joy dribbling down the drainpipe of hard circumstances, you have a choice. You can struggle on your own and hope for the best, or you can focus on God in praise and adoration for who He is. Hebrews 13:15 says, "Through Jesus, therefore, let us continually offer to God a sacrifice of praise—the fruit of lips that openly profess his name."

Work on building a habit pattern of worshiping and praising Him often, whether circumstances are nice or nasty. You won't always feel like it. In fact, it's a sacrifice to praise continually, especially when you don't feel like it. But to do so gives glory to God and joy to you.

When the dry, dusty winds of trials flail you, do your lips bear bitter fruit of complaining and self-pity, or sweet, juicy fruit of praise to the Gardener? Do you only praise Him when you're comfortably enjoying the light, cool rains of blessing? Or do you praise Him even in the dry, difficult times? Your answer to these questions will determine whether you live in joy most of the time, sometimes, or hardly ever. Remember, the choice is yours.

Opening the Door to Joy

Day 1

1. Read "Discovering the Key."

   a. List any new truths you uncovered.

   b. What will you apply from this section?

2. What does Psalm 100:2 tell us to do? (NIV)

   a. Name two ways we are to worship the Lord.

   b. How are you doing at worshiping in these ways? Explain.

3. Using a dictionary, define *worship* and *praise*.

   a. How are they similar?

   b. How are they different?

4. What do you learn about God from the following verses? Meditate on each and use them to worship God. For example, "God is holy." Think about what holy means and how God is holy. Then praise God for His holiness.

   Nehemiah 9:5

   Psalm 59:17

   Psalm 71:22

   Zechariah 14:16

   Romans 9:5

   Revelation 14:7

5. Challenge: List other characteristics of God we are to worship. Use Scriptures, if possible.

6. If you haven't started a list of God's attributes to help you worship Him, begin one now with the characteristics you learn from this chapter. Keep this list in a place you will see often and use it to praise God. Also, if you haven't already done so, go to www.DailyNameofGod. It gives regular reminders to worship our amazing God.

7. How are we to worship? John 4:24; Hebrews 12:28

8. Journal: What is God saying to you today about worship?

Day 2

1. According to these verses, why do we praise or worship God?

   1 Chronicles 16:25

   Psalm 147:1

   Isaiah 63:7

   Ephesians 1:3

2. Challenge: Using Scripture, list other reasons to worship God.

3. Read Luke 24:50-53.

   a. How did the disciples respond to Jesus? verse 52a

   b. What was the result of their response? verse 52b

   c. Then what did they do?

   d. From these verses explain the relationship between joy and worship.

4. Joy is one result of worship. What are other results?

   Exodus 23:25-26

   2 Chronicles 20:21-22

5. How has God worked in your life through worship? If you haven't seen any results, what might be the reason?

6. Worshiping God not only brings joy, it is also an expression of our joy. How is Jesus described in Luke 10:21, and how did He express His joy?

7. Journal: How do you express your joy?

   a. How can you communicate it like Jesus did in Luke 10:21?

   b. Write down some phrases expressing your joy.

Day 3

1. Often when we're happy, we forget to praise God.

   a. What is your typical reaction when you're joyful?

   b. What response is encouraged in James 5:13?

2. Music helps us praise God. The Bible often links music and praise. What do 2 Chronicles 5:13 and Psalm 47:6 say?

3. Joy often accompanies singing and worship as we saw in Psalm 100:2. What does Psalm 95:1-2 say about this?

4. Challenge: Skim through the Psalms and notice the important role of singing. Observe the connection with either praise or joy. What does this say to you?

5. How does music help you worship God?

6. What steps could you take to begin praising God more through music?

7. Journal: Do you experience joy as you praise God through music? Explain.

Day 4

1. What other ways, besides music, can we worship and praise God?

    1 Chronicles 16:29

    Psalm 26:7

    Luke 2:37

    Romans 12:1

    Add other ways:

    a. Which methods help you personally to worship God?

    b. Explain how they help you worship.

2. What inhibits you from worshiping God?

    How can you correct this?

3. Read Psalm 34:1 and 145:1-2.

   a. How long and how often are we to worship God?

   b. How does your worship measure up to these standards established in
      Scripture?

4. Read David's prayer of praise in 1 Chronicles 29:9-13. How did David and
   the people feel in verse 9, immediately after the provision of all the building
   materials for the temple?

   a. How did David respond to his joy in verse 10?

   b. Read verses 10-13 again slowly, meditating on each phrase. Make this your
      prayer to the Lord, writing down phrases that stand out to you.

5. Challenge: Read through the Psalms to learn more about praise and worship.
   Keep a notebook, and record what you learn. As you read, stop and praise
   God for what you discover about Him.

   Write your own psalm of praise to God.

6. Journal: What can you do to begin to worship God more? Perhaps listing specific goals and times you will worship Him would be a good starting point. Share your goals with a friend and ask him/her to check up on you regularly.

Day 5

1. Review this study. What have you learned that will bring you more joy?

2. How will worship deepen your joy?

3. Meditate on and memorize a verse from this week's lesson that will help you find more joy. Write out this verse below.

    What will you do to make this truth come alive for you?

4. Journal: Write a prayer or song of praise and worship to God using some of His characteristics described in this study.

CHAPTER 9

Trials Build Joy

Discovering the Key

What should have been one of the happiest times of my (Gaylyn's) life turned into one of the most difficult. My second son, Daniel, was born with pneumonia and many abnormalities. *Things like this only happened to other people,* I thought. After dozens of tests, six surgeries, and examinations from twenty-five pediatric specialists, the doctors told us Daniel's brain was smaller than usual. But they couldn't predict how it would affect his life—he could be normal or like a vegetable.

For three agonizing months, tears constantly blurred my eyes. Questions raged in my head. *How could a loving God do this to me or my helpless baby? It wasn't fair! What about the future?* Shock, anger, guilt, despair, depression, and self-pity crushed me.

When Daniel developed pneumonia for the fifth time, the doctor told us he didn't have long to live. Mixed emotions flooded my heart. Sadness combined with an indescribable peace and joy overwhelmed me. I had trusted the doctors to heal Daniel, but now realized that neither they nor I could do anything to save him.

Finally, I redirected my trust to God and accepted His plan— whether my son would live or die, whether he would be physically or mentally challenged or normal.

Tim Hansel's book *You Gotta Keep Dancin'* taught me that joy is a choice—in any situation. "Life can be tough," Hansel writes. "Stress, disappointment, heartache, hurt—all are part of the human condition. But while pain is unavoidable, misery is optional." I couldn't choose whether or not to experience pain, but I could choose to be miserable or not. (Hansel, 1985).

For Daniel's first three months, I was miserable because I focused on my situation and my pain. During the next three months, my focus shifted to God, and my misery disappeared. I experienced a never-before-encountered joy. God didn't remove my problems—they were simply less ominous in comparison to His greatness, as my thoughts redirected completely to Him.

Day after day, Daniel's health grew worse. Then, one day, our loving Lord removed his pain and physical deformities and made him perfect. Daniel was with Jesus. Tears mingled with joy.

We rejoiced that Daniel could live forever, pain-free and healthy. But we also grieved because he had touched our family unforgettably, and we missed him.

How can we discover true joy in the midst of difficulties? In chapter 1, we learned joy doesn't come from easy circumstances, but from a deep, settled confidence in our loving Heavenly Father who controls life's details.

While joy and trials are not mutually exclusive, I was amazed that over half of the New Testament references to joy are connected to suffering—either for the writer, the hearers, or both. We can find joy as we experience trials.

First Peter is a letter of suffering, where the idea is mentioned thirty-four times. Yet it's also a letter of joy. In chapter 4, Peter says, "Dear friends, do not be surprised at the fiery ordeal that has come on you to test you, as though something strange were happening to you. But rejoice inasmuch as you participate in the sufferings of Christ, so that you may be overjoyed when his glory is revealed." (verses 12-13). Suffering is a normal part of the Christian life. It shouldn't surprise us. Scripture often tells us how to respond to suffering: "Rejoice." (See Romans 5:3 and James 1:2.)

What kind of trials are you facing—large or small? Sometimes the small ones are the hardest to deal with. Today you can choose to experience joy in your situation through application of each key in this book. Here are some steps that can help you find joy in your trials.

1. *Focus your eyes on God, rather than on your problems.* Where is your focus today? Hebrews 12:2 tells us to fix "our eyes on Jesus, the pioneer and perfecter of our faith." Consider what God has done for you in the past and thank Him. Also, think about who God is—His greatness, love, etc. Then praise and worship Him. When our minds mull over our situations, we can become depressed, angry, or full of self-pity. As our eyes are lifted from our problems and looking to God, He can and will fill us with His joy.

2. *Pray about your situation and prayerfully sort out your feelings.* Philippians 4:6-7 tells us not to worry about anything, but rather to pray about everything. God promises to bring His peace and, ultimately, joy. When we go through hard times, it's natural to experience feelings—including negative ones. The apostle Paul had many feelings, yet he experienced joy. He was "sorrowful, yet always rejoicing" (2 Corinthians 6:10). Ask God to help you to deal with your feelings.

3. *Trust God to handle your situation and wait for Him to work.* In what areas are you

struggling to trust God? God's plan and timing are often quite different from ours. Remember, He is a loving Heavenly Father who controls every detail of life—even though it may not always seem like it. Psalm 33:21 says joy comes as we trust God. To experience a deeper joy in your life, trust God more, especially in the hard times.

4.   *Choose to rejoice in the Lord.* What area do you need to choose to rejoice in today? Philippians 4:4 says, "Rejoice in the Lord always." When our lives are calm, rejoicing is easy. When trials come, we don't feel like rejoicing. But, joy is not a feeling. It's an attitude that requires a conscious choice.

5.   *Find a friend so you can talk, share your feelings, and pray.* Sharing with a friend when you're struggling can bring comfort, encouragement, and joy. Paul experienced all of these through his friendships (2 Corinthians 7:4-13). Do you have a close friend you regularly share and pray with? If not, ask God to bring you that friend, and begin looking for him or her.

We also need to be available to help friends when they go through difficult times. God can use the trials we've been through to bring comfort to friends when they are hurting (2 Corinthians 1:3-4). (See question 5 on day 5 of this chapter for ways to help.)

God wants to give us joy during our trials. It's our choice to either let Him work in us through our trials or to fight Him and be miserable. It took me three months to begin to let God work. If I would have allowed Him to begin immediately, I would not have missed so much joy and peace. Please don't miss the joy God has for you. Begin now to give your trials to God, and let Him give you joy in the midst of them!

Opening the Door to Joy

Day 1

1. Read "Discovering the Key."

   a. List any new truths you uncovered.

   b. What will you apply from this section?

2. According to 1 Peter 1:6-8, what will come into our lives? Why?

   a. How are we to respond? (See also James 1:2-4.)

   b. What quality of joy are we to have?

   c. When have you experienced this joy during a trial?

3. Why do we rejoice in our sufferings? Romans 5:3-5

4. Is suffering normal or abnormal for believers? Philippians 1:29, Romans 8:16-17

5. What are some purposes for suffering?

   Psalm 119:67

2 Corinthians 1:3-11

2 Corinthians 4:10-11

2 Corinthians 12:7-10

6. Challenge: List other purposes of suffering, with Scriptures.

7. What are some results of suffering?

Romans 8:18, 28-29

2 Corinthians 4:17

1 Peter 3:14; 5:10

James 1:12

8. Challenge: List other results of suffering, with Scriptures.

9. Journal: Which results of suffering have you experienced?

a. What has kept you from experiencing others?

b. Which are you looking forward to experiencing? Why?

Day 2

1. List some of Paul's troubles from 2 Corinthians 6:4-10 and 11:23-29.

2. How did Paul describe his troubles in 2 Corinthians 4:16-18?

   a. What are our trials doing for us?

   b. In the middle of trials, where should our focus be? How will this insight help you?

3. What do these examples teach you about emotions and responses to trials?

   David: Psalm 6:2-7, Psalm 56:3-4

   The Apostles: Acts 5:41

   Paul: Acts 16:23-25, 2 Corinthians 2:4; 6:10

   Jesus: Mark 14:33-34, Hebrews 12:2, 1 Peter 2:21-23

   a. Which example speaks to you today?

   b. How and why does it speak to you?

4. What emotions do you feel when suffering, and how do you respond?

In what way are these emotions appropriate in light of the previous examples?

5. Challenge: Read or skim through the book of Job. List Job's sufferings, his reactions, and what he learned from his trials. Also, how did his friends help or hinder him?

6. Journal: What recent trials have slammed joy's door for you?

   a. How could you have kept the door open?

   b. How would the results have been different?

Day 3

1. How are we to respond to God in our trials?

   Psalm 18:6

   Psalm 37:3-7

   Psalm 141:8

   Matthew 11:28

   1 Peter 4:19; 5:7

   James 5:13

2. What other responses should we have during suffering?

   Psalm 31:7

   Romans 12:3,12, 21

   2 Timothy 2:3; 4:5

   Hebrews 10:36

   James 1:2

   1 Peter 4:1, 12-14; 5:7-8

3. Challenge: List other responses to suffering, with Scriptures.

4. List ways we should relate to God's Word during suffering: Psalm 119:50, 61, 78, 81, 92.

5. Which responses are easiest and hardest for you? Why?

6. Read Habakkuk 3:17-18.

   a. How did Habakkuk choose to respond to his trial?

   b. What did he rejoice in?

    c. Rewrite these verses, personalizing them by inserting your own situations. Then choose to rejoice.

7. Journal: Choose one or more trials you wrote about in Day 2. Using some of the responses you studied in Days 2 and 3, prayerfully write what you will begin doing to experience more joy in them.

Day 4

1. What attributes of God can we rely on during suffering?

   2 Chronicles 30:9

   Isaiah 40:25

   Romans 2:4

   2 Corinthians 1:18

2. How does God minister to our emotional and personal needs during trials?

   Psalm 4:7; 43:4

   Psalm 46:1; 68:19

   Isaiah 40:29

   Romans 15:5,13

3. Challenge: List other ways God ministers to us, with Scriptures.

4. Meditate on God's presence with you as you read Psalm 32:8, 10; 91:15; 109:31; and Hebrews 13:5. Write down any meaningful phrases.

    What is God saying to you today?

5. What do the following verses promise?

    Psalm 30:5, 11

    Psalm 94:19

    Psalm 126:5-6

    John 16:20-22

6. Challenge: What other promises can you hold onto during trials?

7. Journal: How and when has God been a resource for you in times of suffering?

    How can you rely on God's attributes and presence even more during difficult times?

Day 5

1. Review this study. What can you take away to help you open joy's door in your trials?

2. Meditate on and memorize a verse from this lesson that will help you find more joy. Write this verse below.

    a. How can you make that truth come alive for you?

    b. Record any new insights the Lord gives you.

3. From what you have learned in this chapter, how should suffering affect your joy?

4. Challenge: Read 1 Peter. What do you learn about suffering and joy?

5. How can you help a friend who is hurting?

    Proverbs 12:25

    Romans 12:15

    Galatians 6:2

    2 Corinthians 1:3-4

    Thessalonians 5:11, 14

James 1:19

Add other ways:

6. Journal: How have you experienced help from a friend when you were suffering?

   a. Who can you reach out to today?

   b. What will you do to help?

Note: For a more complete Bible study on suffering, go to www.RRbooks.org. You'll find a free article called, "A Biblical View of Suffering.

CHAPTER 10

Friendships Increase Joy

Discovering the Key

Bobbie and I will never forget our thirty-fifth anniversary. No, we didn't go to Hawaii or Paris. We just went down from our mountain village in California to Palm Springs for dinner with our best friends, Jim and Jan. But on the way back home a lifelong, joyful memory was built. As we drove up the mountain the clear night sky sparkled like thousands of diamonds, while the city below us shimmered with light. We pulled off the road at a lookout to enjoy the beauty together.

Jim spontaneously shared something special about their marriage. Bobbie mentioned a quality she appreciated in ours. Jan expressed her joy in Jim's faithful love. Soon we were swept away in a stream of gratitude as we took turns uttering words of praise. We celebrated our marriages, our spouses, and our friendship. Feelings of joy long held deep in our hearts, but seldom put into words, were brought to light. Even as I share this story the joy of that night floods over me.

Someone said, "When you share pain with someone you divide it, but when you share joy you multiply it." Sharing our joy that night filled us to overflowing as we felt it multiply.

God designed us to receive joy through our relationships. He wants us to share our lives in the closest possible relationships with others, as long as they are pure and healthy. By pure, I mean that our friendships must not demonstrate even the slightest hint of sexual immorality or impropriety (Ephesians 5:3-4). By healthy, I mean we can receive great joy by being with friends but not becoming dependent on them. Friends should never replace our total dependency on God (Psalm 73:25).

God's Word is all about relationships—with Him and with each other. Next time you read through the Gospels, notice how much Christ's disciples meant to Him personally. He loved to spend time with His best friends.

When I was a Bible translator in Guatemala translating Luke 22 into Chuj, I came to verse 15, where Jesus said, "I have eagerly desired to eat this Passover with you before I suffer." "Eagerly desired" is so strong that it is translated "lust" or "covet" everywhere else in many versions of the New Testament, except in 1 Thessalonians 2. There Paul spoke of his "intense longing" to be with his friends. Jesus and Paul are superb examples of people who developed deep, healthy friendships characterized by joy. Paul went so far as to say, "Indeed, you are our glory and joy" (1 Thessalonians 2:20).

Let me ask you a few personal questions about your relationships. Are your family relationships soaked in joy? If not, what one thing can you begin doing today to pour a little more joy into them?

Do you have one or two friends that are so close you long to be with them when you're separated for a time? Does anything hinder you from diving into such deep relationships?

Resentment pulverizes joy. Do you hold any grudge, even slight, against a friend or family member? Are you willing to let go of it, so joy can replace it? Do you need to humbly ask forgiveness of someone and help them let go of their resentment toward you?

Please don't read further until you've thought through these questions, talked them over with the Lord, and maybe with someone else you trust.

What kinds of things do you do with your family and friends to build joy? Here are five practical ideas we've found helpful. We hope they'll stimulate your creativity in this area.

1. *Share deeply from your heart with one another.* That's not easy, and it takes time to crack open the crust that protects our tender inner being. But whether you're sharing as husband and wife, parent and child, or friend and friend, work at being honest, open, and transparent with each other. In sharing, we've found that the greater the risks, the deeper the joy we experience.

2. *Really listen to one another with your heart.* A sharing heart cries out for a listening heart. When others begin to tell you their trials or joys, do you give yourself wholeheartedly to try to understand and enter into their feelings? Or do you quickly give advice or begin thinking of your own trials or joys, so you can play "Mine's worse (or better) than yours?"

3. *Pray together. Make it a habit to take each other's joys and trials to the Lord, alone as well as together.* Talk with Him, not only about your concerns but also what you appreciate about Him and each other. Praying together can draw you closer to each other and the Lord.

4. *Discover creative ways to encourage each other.* Find out what makes your friend

really feel loved. Can you do those things? They may be as simple as sending a note to say how much you appreciate him or her, or a call asking how you can pray.

5. *Have fun together.* This may sound obvious, but we can easily let our pressured lives eliminate fun times with those we love. When was the last time you went out for breakfast or lunch with your best friend, or took your child on a "date?" We love going out to breakfast together for some father-daughter time.

What are some of the fun activities you used to do with others, but have given up because your schedule is too crowded? Decide to restore some of the joy of doing fun things with people you love to be with.

Joy is like good food. It tastes much better when shared around a table that overflows with love. And it becomes moldy when it's left alone too long. Is your joy stale or moldy today? We encourage you to find a friend and begin developing a deeper friendship.

Opening the Door to Joy

Day 1

1. Read "Discovering the Key."

    a. List any new truths you uncovered.

    b. What will you apply from this section?

2. Read 1 Thessalonians 2:7-13 and 17-20.

    a. Describe Paul's relationship to the believers from verses 7 and 11.

    b. What were his feelings toward them?

    c. How did Paul describe the believers in verses 19-20?

    d. How would you describe your relationships with other believers?

    e. How do your relationships compare with Paul's?

3. Challenge: Answer questions 2a, b, and c, this time based on Philippians 4:1.

4. What do the above passages in 1 Thessalonians and Philippians teach you about relationships?

5. Read 2 Timothy 1:4. Why did Paul long to see Timothy?

6. How should we respond to others? Romans 12:15; Philippians 2:17

7. Journal: Honestly consider your relationships with other Christians. Do they bring you joy? Do others find joy through you? Why or why not? Write your responses.

Day 2

1. Who brings us joy? Or to whom can we bring joy, and how?

Proverbs 10:1; 23:15

Ecclesiastes 9:9

Luke 1:58

Luke 15:6, 9, 32

2. List some things that brought joy and gladness to the believers.

Psalm 42:4

Acts 15:30-31

Romans 16:19

2 John 4

What brings joy and gladness to your heart?

3. What quality of joy can we experience in relationship to others? 3 John 3-4
   In what ways have you experienced this?

4. What will make our joy complete? Philippians 2:2

5. How can we make the work of our leaders (pastors, etc.) a joy and not a
   burden? Philippians 2:29; Hebrews 13:17

6. How did Paul contribute to the believers? Philippians 1:25-26; 2 Corinthians
   1:24

7. Journal: Why did Paul thank God in 1 Thessalonians 3:9?

   a. How often do you do this?

   b. What prevents you from thanking God for others?

   c. Stop right now and make a list of people for whom you thank God. Then
      list those you want to begin thanking Him for.

Day 3

1. What are some wrong ways of relating to others? Write down what is shown
   to be wrong under each passage of Scripture.

   Leviticus 19:11

   Zechariah 7:10

   Romans 1:24-27

   Romans 14:13

   Titus 3:3

James 4:11

   a. What errors in relating to others do you see in your life? Ask the Lord to
      show you how to deal with them.

   b. What helps us avoid such attitudes? 1 Corinthians 6:11

2. Challenge: List additional ways we should not interact with others, using
   Scriptures where possible.

3. List positive ways to relate to others. Look up as many of the following
   Scriptures as time permits.

   John 13:34

   Romans 12:10,16

   Romans 15:7

   1 Corinthians 1:10

   Galatians 5:13

   Ephesians 4:2, 32

   Colossians 3:16

   2 Thessalonians 1:3

   Hebrews 10:24-25

James 5:16

1 Peter 4:8-9

1 Peter 5:5

4. Look back over this list and meditate on each action.

   a. Which are you putting into practice? How?

   b. Which do you need to work on?

   c. How do you plan to improve today?

5. Journal: How will interacting with other Christians in positive ways bring you joy? Share a time you experienced this.

Day 4

1. In Philemon 7, what did Philemon do for Paul? How?

2. What does 1 Thessalonians 5:11 command us to do?

   a. Give practical, personal examples showing how to do this.

   b. How have others encouraged you?

3. How are we to encourage others? 2 Timothy 4:2b

4. How often should we encourage others and why? Hebrews 3:13

   a. How often do you encourage those close to you?

    b. In what ways do you spur them on?

5. Read 2 Chronicles 32:1-8.

    a. How did Hezekiah encourage the people?

    b. What can you apply from Hezekiah's example?

6. What's the connection between joy and encouragement? Is one dependent on the other?

7. Journal: Who in your life needs encouragement today?

    a. What specifically will you do to encourage them?

    b. Personalize Isaiah 50:4 and write it as your prayer.

Day 5

1. Review this study.

    a. How has God spoken to you in this chapter?

    b. What will you take away that will increase your joy?

2. In what ways have relationships increased your joy?

3. How are you bringing joy to others?

4. Meditate on and memorize a verse from this lesson that will help you find more joy. Write out the verse below.

   What will you do to make that truth spring to life for you?

5. Journal: What keeps you from experiencing more joy in your relationships with other believers? Record what you can do to increase your joy.

CHAPTER 11

An Attitude Check Unbinds Joy

Discovering the Key

As a child, I didn't fit in with the children around me. Those feelings of insecurity gnawed at my fragile self-esteem. Why couldn't I be like others, who seemed so self-assured and at ease?

Have you ever felt this way? Such insecurities may have robbed you of some of the joy of childhood, just as they did me. They possibly still plague you.

Becoming a joyful person involves looking inside and understanding oneself. It means dealing with destructive attitudes (which rob us of joy), then building healthy attitudes. In Matthew 22:37-40, Jesus spoke of three relationships: with God, others, and ourselves. He said each must be bathed in love and is necessary for our full joy.

We've already looked at our relationship with the Lord and with others. Now let's consider how our relationship to ourselves determines our joy. Here are three important steps that lead us to experience the full joy Jesus intended.

1. *Accept yourself and others as God's unique creations.* The apostles were radically different from each other. Thomas—pessimistic. James and John—enthusiastic, energetic, and eager to gain status. Peter—sometimes exuberant and sometimes in the dumps. Yet the Lord created and chose each one.

Each of us is different, and we express our joy differently. Some of us radiate joy like the sun. We're naturally bubbly and look on the bright side of things. Others of us are quieter and more subdued, keeping our feelings to ourselves. We may think we don't have as much joy as others because it doesn't show as much.

The good news is that God made each of us to experience joy in our own unique ways. Quiet, subtle joy can be as real and powerful as exploding exuberance. We shouldn't condemn anyone, including ourselves, as unspiritual just because we don't express joy like others.

Whatever our temperament, each of us has the same potential for having Christ's joy. I'm glad Jesus didn't put any qualifiers in John 16:24. It doesn't take a gushing personality to have complete joy!

2. *Recognize that no one bubbles over with joy every minute of every day.* Difficulties touch everyone, and it's not unspiritual to hurt. David often cried out in despair (see Psalm 43). We can identify with David when our Christian lives bounce from moments of heart-rending despair to indescribable joy.

Many things can temporarily hinder us from choosing joy: physical problems, stress, disappointment, painful relationships, depression, anxiety, or overwhelming grief. Our pilgrimage may be a struggle, but we can remain on the road to joy. Quickly choosing to rejoice can keep our feelings from taking control.

The apostle Paul is a good example of one who experienced great emotional pain in his life and ministry. Second Corinthians describes some of his struggles: "Great distress and anguish of heart and with many tears" (2:4), "perplexed" (4:8), "burdened" (5:4), "downcast" (7:6), and "afraid" (7:5; 11:3).

In the midst of great strain, he experienced joy! This duality is clearly illustrated in his amazing statement in 2 Corinthians 6:10: "Sorrowful, yet always rejoicing." During the hard times, Paul found the strength to rejoice because he fixed his eyes on what is unseen—Jesus and His work (4:18). When joy is a difficult choice, it helps to focus on Jesus. In time, joy will come from the Lord.

If we're struggling with a lack of joy, we may be carrying burdens God wants us to discard. Hebrews 12:1 encourages us to "throw off everything that hinders and the sin that so easily entangles." We need to ask ourselves: "What hindrances and/or sins are robbing me of joy today?" In the power of Christ, we can begin to throw off the hindrances by giving them to Him. As we do, our burdens lighten, and we can focus more intently on Jesus—the Creator of joy.

This doesn't mean we'll never feel sad, troubled, disappointed, or grieved. The ocean illustrates how the Lord made us to respond on two levels. The ocean has surface currents and deep water currents. On one level, the winds of circumstance toss the surface waves of the ocean. On the surface, our emotions carry us from the heights of delight to the depths of despair—sometimes between heartbeats!

The second level of the ocean is in its depths. Storms don't easily affect the depths of the sea. Down deep, joy can reign consistently. Joy isn't an emotion that rises with good times and falls with bad. Instead, it is like a strong current far below the ocean's surface. Joy wells to the surface at times, but its strength comes from deep within.

3. *Another step to inner joy is having personal freedom to rejoice.* Do you need permission to be joyful? Many Christians live joyless lives because they believe they have no right to joy. At least five factors may keep us from living joyfully.

First, weaknesses can rob us of joy, if we say, "Until I conquer this weakness, I'll never be content." Let's learn to imitate Paul's joyful response to weaknesses in 2 Corinthians 12:9-10. (See day 2 of this study.)

Second, sins from the past and mistakes can weigh us down and crush our joy. Christ died to give us joy! He took all our sins on Himself so that in His righteousness we have a right to joy.

The third area in which our joy is robbed involves false guilt or a bondage to legalism. Knowing that God loves us isn't enough. Instead, we trap ourselves into doing things to earn God's acceptance. But we can never do enough or be good enough apart from His grace. The Galatian Christians were trying to do this when Paul asked them in 4:15, "What has happened to all your joy?"

Fourth, childhood experiences can rob us of permission to be joyful. In my home, open expression of joy was discouraged. I was often reprimanded whenever I laughed loudly, sang, or openly demonstrated my joy. As a young boy, I thought expressing joy wasn't appropriate since it made others uncomfortable. Whenever it reared its "ugly" head, I consciously squelched it! After finding Christ as an adult, it took years to overcome the condemning inner voice that said, "It's not OK to be too joyful or openly express it." What unconscious messages inhibit your joy?

A word to parents: Do you cherish your children's resonant, joyful noises around the home? Or do you squelch their joy because you want peace and quiet at all times?

Fifth, when others are joyless, we may not feel free to rejoice. The awful conditions of those suffering deprivation in the world can rob joy. Jesus also lived in a society filled with suffering people. He responded with compassion but didn't allow their suffering to rob Him of joy. We may feel we have no right to joy when someone we love is hurting because of illness, death, divorce, financial ruin, or childhood abuse. Each of these situations causes great pain, but they don't eliminate our right to rejoice in the Lord.

We can help others in practical ways: comforting, encouraging, strengthening, and praying for them. But we can't let their pain drown us in misery. Again, Jesus is our example. Just before leaving His own mother and brothers, knowing they would grieve over His death, He talked of the full measure of His joy (John 17:13).

This study will guide you through Hebrews 12:1-3 and examine areas that may close your door to joy while seeking ways you can open that door wider.

Before moving on, consider each step to inner joy. Is your relationship with yourself strong enough that joy's door regularly opens wide for you? Ask the Lord to reveal any ways you may be robbing yourself of the joy He wants for you. If He reveals any, start working toward ways to alleviate them. Ask Him to reveal new, healthy ways to relate to yourself that will bring you greater joy.

Opening the Door to Joy

Day1

1. Read "Discovering the Key."

    a. List any new truths you uncovered.

    b. What will you choose to apply from this section?

2. What did Jesus want for His disciples in John 17:13?

    a. What did He mean?

    b. Has this ever been your experience? Explain.

3. Read 2 Corinthians 6:3-10.

    a. What does Paul contrast in verse 10a?

    b. How can we experience both qualities at the same time?

    c. Give an example.

4. Challenge: What trials did Paul and his companions endure in 2 Corinthians 6:3-10 and 11:23-29? How did they respond?

5. Read and begin to memorize Hebrews 12:1-3. List four commands you find.

6. What does Hebrews 12:1 tell us to throw off? How do these rob our joy?

7. How does sin entangle us?

   Is it instant or gradual? Explain, with an example, if possible.

8. Write what 1 John 1:8-9 tells us. Then confess your sins, ask God's forgiveness, and pray for the Lord's help to flee temptation.

9. Journal: What things do you need to throw off today that are robbing your joy? Ask God to reveal them to you.

   a. What sins have entangled you in the past or present?

   b. What could you have done to avoid them?

Day 2

1. Read 2 Corinthians 12:7-10. Paul reveals a hindrance and a major potential joy killer—weaknesses.

   a. What weakness do you struggle with?

   b. How are those weaknesses affecting your joy?

2. Which kills your joy the most, the weakness itself or your attitude toward the weakness? Explain.

3. Second Corinthians 12 gives three steps for dealing with our weaknesses.

   a. What's the first step to deal with a weakness? verse 8

   b. What did Jesus say in verse 9? Write out and meditate on this second step.

   c. What is God saying to you through it?

   d. The third step is to joyfully accept our weaknesses. In verses 9b-10, what did Paul do and why?

4. Challenge: Write your own definition of weakness or look it up in a dictionary.

   Then study what the Word says about weaknesses, beginning with Romans 8:26; 1 Corinthians 1:27; 2:3; and Hebrews 4:15. Summarize what you learn.

5. Journal: Prayerfully begin to deal with one weakness using the steps from 2 Corinthians 12. Ask God to reveal how your weakness can bring you joy.

Day 3

1. What is the second command given in Hebrews 12:1?

   What does it mean?

2. Define perseverance. Explain how we run with this quality.

3. How is the Christian life like a race? Is it more like a sprint or a marathon? Explain.

4. List insights from Galatians 5:7 and Philippians 3:14 for running this race.

5. What does God give us according to Romans 15:5?

   Share a time you experienced this.

6. How does 1 Corinthians 9:24-27 tell us to run? In practice how do we do it?

7. How does 1 Corinthians 9:26 tell us not to run?

   a. What are some ways we run like this? Give personal examples.

   b. How can we keep from running this way?

8. How do 1 Corinthians 9:25a and 27a say we prepare for our race?

   a. How do we do these two things in the Christian life?

   b. Contrast the physical and the spiritual runner and race.

9. How did Paul describe his race? 2 Timothy 4:7-8

   a. What reward did Paul anticipate? verse 8

   b. If this were the end of your life, could you say the same? If not, what could you begin doing today?

10. Journal: How is God speaking to you today about running the Christian race? What steps of action will you take?

Day 4

1. What do Hebrews 12:2a and 3a tell us to do?

   a. What do these last two commands mean to you?

   b. Explain practically how you can apply them.

   c. What does Psalm 105:3-4 add? What result is in verse 3?

2. The Greek word for "fix our eyes" or "looking unto" means not only looking toward something (Jesus), but also looking away from something.

   a. What do you need to look away from today so you can look to Jesus?

   b. Write a prayer asking God to help you focus on Him and turn your eyes away from other hindrances in your life.

3. What does Colossians 3:1-3 tell us to do and why?

   How can you put this into action?

4. Challenge: How is Jesus described in Hebrews 12:2?

   a. What did He endure for us?

   b. Where was His focus?

c. Why is it important for you to focus there?

5. Extra Challenge: Read one or more accounts of Jesus' suffering: Matthew 26-27; Mark 14-15; Luke 22-23; John 18-19; or Isaiah 53. Use a separate sheet to answer the following:

   a. Note each area of suffering and how Christ responded.

   b. Which area do you think was most difficult for Him?

   c. Which would be most difficult for you?

   d. How can the Author and Finisher of your faith help you?

6. Why are we to consider Jesus? Hebrews 12:3b.

   a. If you feel this way today, what is the remedy?

   b. How can you apply it?

7. Which command in Hebrews 12:1-3 is hardest for you? Why?

   How can you work on that area?

8. Journal: Focus your eyes on Jesus now. Using your list of Jesus' characteristics, begun in chapter 2, write your thanks and praise to Him.

Day 5

1. Review this week's study. What can you take away from this study that will bring you more joy?

2. Review the steps to inner joy, given in "Discovering the Key." Which do you need to work on? How will you begin?

3. How does Hebrews 12:1-3 relate to your joy?

    If you follow the instructions, in what ways will you have more joy?

4. Meditate on and memorize Hebrews 12:1-2. What will make these truths come alive for you?

5. Journal: What *internal* struggles may be locking you out of joy? These may include destructive attitudes, unrealistic expectations, or unresolved feelings such as anger, grief, guilt, or fear.

    Choose one of these, and write specifically what you can begin doing to find joy in it. For example, begin giving the struggle to Him when you're aware of it, and tell Him you trust Him to take it, in His time.

CHAPTER 12

Gratitude Encourages Joy

Discovering the Key

The situation couldn't have been worse. I felt miserable in the sweltering heat. After nine wonderful days ministering to missionaries in the high mountains of Pakistan, I squeezed into a minibus going to Islamabad to begin the twenty-four-hour trip home. When I got to the broiling hot airport, it was packed with a mass of elbowing, shoving people. At the reservation desk, they said I didn't have a reservation for the flight. The standby list looked discouragingly long, but it was worth a try.

After two blistering hours, the flight was ready. They called name after name on the standby list. I was about to lose hope when my name was called. But my joy evaporated when the clerk said, "Oh, you're going to Karachi. Sorry, we're only taking standbys to the first stop, Lahore. Maybe you can fly tomorrow." I was stunned. I knew no one in Islamabad. I didn't speak the language. I had no place to stay and no money or credit card. To make matters worse, I would miss all connecting flights to the U.S.

Close to despair, I walked away from the counter. Immediately the Lord brought to mind a verse, Zephaniah 3:17. I'd been meditating on it during the trip. It says, "The Lord your God is with you, he is mighty to save. He will take great delight in you, he will quiet you with his love, he will rejoice over you with singing." Forget that verse! I'd rather stew in my misery. But the Lord wouldn't let me off that easy.

Prompted by Him, I decided I wouldn't let my situation control me. So I found a seat in the corner of that stifling room and began to express my gratitude to God for the wonderful truths from that Scripture. I admit that I didn't feel like thanking God. But I decided to keep doing it until the Lord aligned my feelings with the reality of His truth. I praised Him in my heart and expressed my thanks to Him. After a little while God began to remove my wretched frustration and self-pity and to replace it with genuine joy—a joy completely independent of my circumstances!

After at least twenty minutes of praising God, the unbelievable happened. My name was called. I thought the plane had already left, but the clerk said, "Oh, I'm glad you're still here. I called Lahore, and they said you could go on this flight." I was so glad I didn't leave the airport in despair!

I don't know if the Lord answered in response to my gratitude. But, to my surprise, getting on the plane didn't really matter that much anymore. God's joy had completely replaced my frustration. Do you find that hard to believe? If you've experienced God's powerful joy in difficult situations, you don't. If you haven't experienced it, I hope you will soon.

Did you know that the Bible never commands us to *feel* grateful? God knows that our feelings follow our actions. He tells us to give thanks, knowing that as we do this we will begin to feel thankful if we continue to do so.

Like worship, gratitude has a special connection to joy. A godly response when we're joyful is to express gratitude to the Lord for His goodness. So joy often creates gratitude. But the opposite is also true—gratitude generates joy. The second truth, that gratitude brings joy, is difficult to grasp and even more difficult to practice in our lives.

Gratitude is the key that releases joy in our lives. I don't completely understand why. When we give God thanks, He gives us joy. Gratitude opens a wonderful pipeline to God. When our thanks are lifted up to Him, He pours down joy. It's an easy principle to forget. When situations snatch away our joy, we feel like doing anything except thanking God—but that's exactly what we need to do.

Ann Voskamp explains it this way in *One Thousand Gifts*: "While I may not always feel joy, God asks me to give thanks in all things, because He knows that the *feeling* of joy begins in the action of thanksgiving" (Voskamp, 2011).

I've been working on building a habit pattern of responding with thanksgiving when I feel joyless, particularly when situations rob my joy. It's not easy, and I have a long way to go. But every time I do it, I'm glad.

The little "joy robbers" are often more of a challenge than the big ones. They sneak in and plunder our joy so subtly that it's difficult to realize what's happening.

One night when we lived in Idyllwild, CA, I was coming back from a long trip. Just a few miles from home I was driving up our narrow mountain road about midnight. I didn't see the jagged boulder in the road until too late, and it demolished one of my front tires.

As I climbed out of the car, those familiar repulsive feelings of frustration and self-pity drenched me. Then I stopped. I could make a choice—either continue feeling miserable or thank God. Rather than get the spare tire out immediately, I stood beside the road thanking God for everything I could think of. I began with my safety and ended with some of His wonderful characteristics.

Within a few minutes, God filled my heart with His joy. I changed the tire and went on my way rejoicing. That experience makes me want to choose joy more often.

What is our motivation for thanking God? It must not be merely to get His joy. That would be selfish, maybe even an attempt to manipulate God into giving us what we want. Our thanks must come out of a heart of genuine gratitude to Him, regardless of our immediate feelings. God then responds by filling our hearts with His joy.

What about you, dear friend? I pray this chapter will encourage you to choose gratitude in your difficult situations. When you choose it from a heartfelt appreciation for the Lord, you'll find that you've chosen joy rather than misery. Gratitude is like any other habit in life. Each time you express it, you'll find it's a little easier the next time.

Opening the Door to Joy

Day 1

1. Read "Discovering the Key."

   a. List any new truths you uncovered.

   b. What will you choose to apply from this section?

2. What action accompanied joy in Psalm 28:7; Isaiah 51:3 and Jeremiah 30:19?

3. How did the people in Psalm 42:4 go to God's house?

   What is your attitude as you go into God's house?

4. Use a dictionary to define gratitude.

5. The Greek word for "give thanks" is *Eucharisteo*. It comes from the Greek word for grace, which comes from the word for joy, *Kara*. Think about how giving thanks could possibly bring joy. Look up the following verses to see the connection between giving thanks and joy:

   Psalm 33:11

   Psalm 95:2 (ESV)

   Psalm 100:1

   Colossians 1:12

6. Is gratitude merely a feeling, or must it include action? Explain.

7. What three actions do we know are God's will for us in 1 Thessalonians 5:16-18? Note: These verses are one sentence in Greek.

   a. How do they relate to each other?

   b. Which is hardest for you? Why?

8. Journal: Begin a gratitude list, on a separate sheet or at the back of this workbook, with things you are thankful for today. Include areas you may not feel thankful for. As you list each one, thank God for them. Add to this list regularly.

Day 2

1. What did the people fail to do in Romans 1:21-24? What was the result?

2. List the hindrances to thankfulness you find in Psalm 106.

   a. Which hindrances do you struggle with?

   b. What can you do to change?

   c. Where was the people's focus?

3. To be filled with joy, where should our focus be?

   Psalm 126:2-3 (also Joel 2:21)

   Acts 14:17

   Hebrews 12:2

4. For what should we thank God?

   Matthew 14:19

   John 11:41

   2 Corinthians 2:14; 9:15

   1 Timothy 1:12

5. Challenge: List other things we should thank God for, with Scriptures, if possible.

6. What results from thanksgiving?

   Psalm 69:30-31

   2 Corinthians 4:15

   Hebrews 12:28 (NIV)

7. What two things does Psalm 107:22 tell us to do?

   a. When is giving thanks a sacrifice?

   b. How is it like an offering?

   c. How can you practice these today?

9. How should feelings and moods affect thankfulness? Explain.

10. Share a time you were able to thank God when you didn't feel like it. What was the result?

11. Journal: List situations that require sacrifice for you to thank God. Thank God for them, regardless of your feelings. What was the result?

Day 3

1. Why are we to give thanks to the Lord?

    Psalm 7:17

    Psalm 107:31

    Psalm 118:1, 21

2. List ways we can thank God, beginning with Psalm 147:7.

3. Read Philippians 1:3-5 and 1 Thessalonians 3:9.

    a. How did Paul pray?

    b. What guide does this give you as you pray for others?

4. What did Paul urge in 1 Timothy 2:1-4 and why?

   What does verse 3 say?

5. What attitudes should accompany prayer? Philippians 4:6-7; Colossians 4:2

6. List things you can thank God for in other believers' lives. Begin with 2 Thessalonians 2:13.

7. When and how often should we give thanks to God?

   1 Chronicles 23:30

   Psalm 35:18

   Psalm 119:62

   Daniel 6:10

   Colossians 1:3

   1 Thessalonians 2:13

8. Challenge: Read Nehemiah 12:24-43.

   a. Why and how were the people celebrating?

   b. What will help your joy and thanksgiving?

9. How thankful are we to be according to Colossians 2:7?

10. List specific times and ways you can begin to show more gratitude to God.

11. Journal: Meditate on Ephesians 5:20. How often are you thankful? How does this verse challenge you?

Day 4

1. Colossians 3:15-17 lists ways to live in relation to other Christians and God. Thanksgiving is mentioned three times. What does that say to you?

2. What should and should not characterize our speech with others? Ephesians 5:4

3. Why is gratitude an important attitude?

4. What are some ways you can show gratitude to others?

5. Write down what you learn about gratitude from:

    a. Naomi's example in Ruth 2:19-20.

    b. Paul's example in Romans 16:1-4.

6. How can we help to develop gratitude in our children or in others around us?

7. Journal: Who do you need to express your gratitude to today?

    a. List people who've had an impact on your life.

Day 5

1. Review this study.

a. How has God spoken to you specifically this week?

b. What can you take away that will bring you more joy?

2. What have you discovered about the relationship between joy and gratitude?

3. How has gratitude encouraged your joy in the past? Give an example.

4. Write your reaction to the statement, "Gratitude unexpressed is ingratitude."

5. Meditate on and memorize a verse from this lesson that will help you find more joy. Write out that verse below.

   How will you make that truth spring to life for you?

6. Journal: Write a prayer asking God to help you be more grateful to Him and to others.

   What can you begin doing to increase your gratitude?

CHAPTER 13

Review Cements Joy

Discovering the Key

Writing this book has challenged our honesty. Repeatedly we've each wondered, *Am I living out the joy I'm encouraging others to choose?* More than once our answer has been "No." We are growing, though, and we hope you are too. As you've worked your way through this book, you've no doubt realized joy isn't something you get once and for all, like salvation. It's more like godliness. It's a quality of life which must be constantly sought after and fought for in life's battlegrounds.

We trust you've gotten the message that if we're walking with Christ we can choose to rejoice in any circumstance. God has provided us with the keys to walk with joy along life's journey. As we walk through life, we choose whether or not to use those keys to open joy's door.

If you've studied through this book, applying what you've learned, you've taken some giant steps toward a life filled with joy. The journey has just begun! Many enemies to joy lurk along the way. Satan hates to see joy glowing in the hearts of God's children. He takes great pains to rob us of it because he knows our joy is a wall of safety around us (Philippians 3:1). Often he doesn't have to bother us, though, because life's circumstances are more than enough to snatch away our joy, if we're not alert.

Be thankful that joy is our birthright in Christ! God desires to fill us continually to overflowing with His joy.

Before we leave this study and continue our journey, let's take one last look at our keys to joy. As we do, we challenge you to renew your commitment to apply these keys and make each a greater part of your life.

1. We have a choice to rejoice! Joy is both our privilege and our duty. True joy comes from no other source. Our Heavenly Father loves to see His children rejoicing, and He makes it possible for us to choose joy, no matter what our circumstances. Are your attempts to find joy centered in the Lord?

2. Our joy must be founded in a heart-knowledge of God. As we get to know Him better, we grow in our ability to choose joy. Getting the facts of who God is from our heads into our hearts is a lifelong process. We need to become experts at this process through consciously working at it. One wonderful result will be an ever-increasing flow of joy at the deepest level of our beings. Is this true of your life right now?

3. A growing knowledge of God's Word is essential to our joy. Our love for God and desire to fellowship with Him should motivate us to spend time in the Word. God's Word not only teaches us how to get joy, but it's also a powerful source of joy in itself. It is God's special, personal love letter to each of us, and nothing brings joy like a love letter. The One who inhabits eternity, who spoke everything into existence, has spoken to us because He loves us so deeply. Should we not take time to listen? Is your time in God's Word a source of joy in your life?

4. Joy and trusting God are inseparable. Without trust in Him, every frustration and predicament snatches away our joy. Our trust protects us from becoming helpless victims of circumstance. Through faith, we see God's faithfulness. As we choose to trust Him, we stand victorious over the potential joy-killers of our lives. Is your trust in God bringing you joy today?

5. Joy is one of the Holy Spirit's fruit (Gal. 5:22-23). As we get to know the Spirit and allow Him to work in our lives, we will experience more and more joy. Just as Jesus relied on the Holy Spirit when He was on earth, we too need to learn to rely on Him. And as we do, we also will experience the full joy Jesus had (Luke 10:21). Does your relationship with the Holy Spirit bring you joy?

6. Joy is a free gift from God to His children, but it can only be received through obeying Him. Disobedience tears our souls apart and slaughters our joy. But obedience heals our damaged souls and opens the way for God to lavish His joy on us. If you're struggling with a shortage of joy, check out your submission to God first. If that's in order, then work on other areas to restore your joy. Is your life so submitted to God that His joy flows into you without restraint?

7. Our Heavenly Father eagerly waits for us to share our hearts with Him through prayer—our gratitude, our sorrows, our needs, our wants, our fears, and our trust. He also longs for us to talk to Him about the needs of others, and through the apostle Paul, He gives us some beautiful models for praying.

We find joy in our Heavenly Father as we become like a child who delights to sit on Daddy's lap and chat. God ministers His joy to our hearts as we talk with Him and as we see Him answer. Is talking with your Father a fountain of joy for you these days?

8. Worship expresses true joy and we find true joy through worship. When joy lifts our hearts, our most appropriate response is to worship the Creator of joy. When our hearts are burdened, we can find joy through worshiping the One who gives His joy to those who love Him. Do you worship God when you're joyful, as well as when you need joy?

9. The world says trials inevitably cheat us of joy. It says, "You can't suffer and have joy too." God's thundering response is, "That's a lie!" Repeatedly His Word teaches us that in His power we can choose joy in the midst of trials. This doesn't deny the reality of grief. Jesus said, "You will grieve, but your grief will be turned to joy" (John 16:20). How often do you come through life's trials with joy as your prize?

10. God made us to experience joy in relationship with others. Our joy is multiplied as our souls are intimately interwoven with those God brings into our lives. Do your friendships generate joy?

11. Our attitudes and responses to ourselves unbind joy in our lives. If we want joy, we must 1) accept ourselves as the unique persons we are, 2) allow ourselves to hurt, knowing that our joy runs deeper than our emotions, and 3) work on resolving any personal hindrances to joy. Are you free to have all the joy God wants to give you?

12. Gratitude is closely related to worship; it voices our joy and it also creates **joy**. It's impossible to consistently thank God in every circumstance and remain joyless! We challenge you to try it. We express gratitude so we can bring joy to God. God then responds by imparting joy to us. Is gratitude such an important part of your life that you can't help but rejoice?

13. You've persevered almost to the end! We pray as you finish this study on joy you'll never be the same. Our desire for you, dear friend, is that your heart will so overflow with joy that it will drench everyone around you. And may your joy not only draw you closer to Christ, may it also be a powerful magnet to draw others to Him.

Opening the Door to Joy

Day 1

1. Read "Discovering the Key."

    a. List any new truths you uncovered.

    b. What will you apply from this section?

2. As you think about the entire study on joy, what impressed you the most?

3. Specifically, how has your door to joy been unlocked through this study?

4. Review chapter 1.

    a. What did you learn about finding joy's door?

    b. What have you been applying?

    c. List areas from chapter 1 where you want to grow more. Specifically, how can you improve in those areas?

d. What Scripture(s) stood out to you and why?

e. Review your memory verse. How is this verse helping you find more joy?

5. Review chapter 2.

a. How has knowing God helped unlock your joy?

b. What have you been applying?

c. List areas from chapter 2 where you want to grow. Specifically, how can you improve in those areas?

d. What Scripture(s) stood out to you and why?

e. Review your memory verse. How is it helping you find more joy?

6. Journal: How have chapters 1 and 2 helped open your door to joy?

Day 2

1. Review chapter 3.

   a. How has God's Word revealed and brought you joy?

   b. What have you been applying?

   c. List areas from chapter 3 where you want to grow. Specifically, how can you improve in those areas?

   d. What Scripture(s) stood out to you and why?

   e. Review your memory verse. How is it helping you find more joy?

2. Review chapter 4.

   a. How has trust released your joy?

   b. What have you been applying?

c. List areas from chapter 4 in which you want to grow more. Specifically, how can you improve in those areas?

d. What Scripture(s) stood out to you and why?

e. Review your memory verse. How is it helping you find more joy?

3. Review chapter 5.

a. What truths about the Holy Spirit encouraged your joy?

b. What have you been applying?

c. List areas from chapter 5 in which you want to grow more.

Specifically, how can you improve in those areas?

d. What Scripture(s) stood out to you and why?

e. Review your memory verse. How is this verse helping you find more joy?

4. Journal: How have chapters 4 and 5 helped open your door to joy?

What areas do you most need work in these chapters?

Day 3

1. Review chapter 6.

a. How has obedience restored your joy?

b. What have you been applying?

c. List areas from chapter 6 in which you want to grow more. Specifically, how can you improve in those areas?

d. What Scripture(s) stood out to you and why?

e. Review your memory verse. How is it helping you find more joy?

2. Review chapter 7.

    a. How has prayer helped maintain your joy?

    b. What have you been applying?

    c. List areas from chapter 7 in which you want to grow more. Specifically, how can you improve in those areas?

    d. What Scripture(s) stood out to you and why?

    e. Review your memory verse. How is it helping you find more joy?

3. Review chapter 8.

    a. How has worship unleashed your joy?

    b. What have you been applying?

   c. List areas from chapter 8 in which you want to grow more. Specifically, how can you improve in those areas?

   d. What Scripture(s) stood out to you and why?

   e. Review your memory verse. How is it helping you find more joy?

4. Journal: How have chapters 6, 7 and 8 helped open your door to joy?

    What areas do you most need work in these chapters?

Day 4

1. Review chapter 9

    a. What did you learn about trials that helped build your joy?

    b. What have you been applying?

    c. List areas from chapter 9 in which you want to grow more. Specifically, how can you improve in those areas?

    d. What Scripture(s) stood out to you and why?

    e. Review your memory verse. How is it helping you find more joy?

2. Review chapter 10.

    a. How have friendships increased your joy?

    b. What have you been applying?

    c. List areas from chapter 10 in which you want to grow more. Specifically, how can you improve in those areas?

    d. What Scripture(s) stood out to you and why?

    e. Review your memory verse. How is it helping you find more joy?

3. Review chapter 11.

    a. What healthy attitudes helped unbind your joy?

    b. What have you been applying?

    c. List areas from chapter 11 in which you want to grow more. Specifically, how can you improve those areas?

    d. What Scripture(s) stood out to you and why?

    e. Review your memory verse. How is this verse helping you find more joy?

4. Journal: How have chapters 9, 10 and 11 helped open your door to joy?

What areas do you most need work in these chapters?

Day 5

1. Review chapter 12.

   a. What truths about gratitude encouraged your joy?

   b. What have you been applying?

   c. List areas from chapter 12 in which you want to grow more. Specifically, how can you improve in those areas?

   d. What Scripture(s) stood out to you and why?

   e. Review your memory verse. How is this verse helping you find more joy?

2. Journal: How has chapter 12 helped open your door to joy?

3. What impacted you most through this study? Explain.

4. What areas are you currently working on?

5. Contrast your joy now versus before you began this study.

6. Journal: What do you need to do to open your door to joy more? List specific steps, then write a prayer asking God to help you. Share your plan with a friend who can encourage you to follow through.

Appendices

Topics for Further Study

The following is a list of topics for further study about joy. Begin with these verses and topics, then add others. On a separate page, or in your journal, write down what you learn about each and how you can apply the principles you glean.

Is there something you need to:
- obey?
- thank or praise God for?
- share with others?

1. God rejoicing:

Psalm 104:31

Isaiah 65:19

Jeremiah 32:41; 33:9

Zephaniah 3:17

Luke 10:21

John 3:29; 15:11; 17:13

2. Nature rejoicing:

1 Chronicles 16:31-33

Job 38:7

Psalms 65:12-13; 66:1; 89:12; 96:11-12; 97:1; 98:4, 8

Isaiah 35:1-2, 6; 44:23; 49:13; 55:12

3. God giving joy as a gift:

Ezra 6:22

Nehemiah 12:43

Job 8:21

Psalms 14:7; 16:11; 45:7

Isaiah 9:3

Acts 14:17

Romans 15:13

4. Notice the contrasts between joy and other things:

Proverbs 10:1, 28; 11:10; 12:20; 14:10, 13; 21:15; 29:2-3, 6

Isaiah 51:11; 61:3, 7; 65:13-14; 66:14

Jeremiah 31:13

John 16:20

1 Corinthians 12:26

2 Corinthians 6:10; 8:2

James 4:9

1 Peter 1:6

5. Go back and do the challenge questions or add to those you've already completed.

6. Do a "subject study" (see chapter 3) on joy or on any topic covered in this book.

Leader's Guide

Leading a group discussion is a rewarding experience. It can also be frightening, especially if it's your first time. By giving specific suggestions, this guide will help facilitate group discussion. As you prepare and lead the group, remember 2 Corinthians 12:9: "My grace is sufficient for you, for my power is made perfect in weakness." Accept His grace and power to lead your group.

Personal Preparation for Each Lesson

1. Pray that God will give wisdom and guidance as you study to learn everything He wants to teach you personally, as well as to effectively lead the discussion. Also pray for God to give all group members understanding and excitement as they study.
2. Do all the homework, highlighting any questions you would like to discuss in the group.
3. Read each chapter's objective in this leader's guide. Consider how the study questions work to accomplish that purpose. Then strive to get that purpose across to the group.
4. Each week specific questions will be listed to help you reach the heart of the lesson and stimulate group discussion. Sometimes extra questions or comments will be added to help you. Highlight these on your study and write in any extra information. In case time is short, the questions in parentheses can be left out. You may want to mark others to possibly leave out.
5. For variation or when time is short, begin with the questions in day 5 to give an overview of the lesson. Then go back to the other days.

Leading the Study

1. Start and end on time. Begin each class with prayer.
2. Encourage members to finish their personal study each week, so they can get the most out of the study and have something to share with others. But remember, you are not there to police their homework. If people don't want to do it, that is their choice. They are the ones who will miss the extra blessing. Don't make them feel guilty or unimportant because they didn't do it. If a person consistently doesn't do the homework, you may want to talk to him/her outside of class to see what may be preventing them.
3. In the first session, as well as whenever anyone new begins the class, tell everyone that everything shared in the study is completely confidential. Get an agreement from participants that they will not share outside the group, anything they hear in the group—including talking to each other about another member, when they are not present.
4. Encourage each member to participate but be sensitive to the shy ones. Never call on anyone who has not volunteered to share. Wait until they are ready to talk, otherwise the group may feel unsafe to those who are more introverted.
5. Keep the discussion on track, bringing it back to the questions when it begins to get off.
6. Act as a moderator, allowing participants to answer the questions. You can share your thoughts, but don't dominate the discussion. If necessary, rephrase the question, but don't be afraid of silence. People may need time to think about their answers.
7. Encourage several people to answer each question by asking, "What do the rest of you think?" or "Anything else?"
8. When a question has several Scriptures listed, ask, "Which verse ministered to you or stood out to you?"
10. Never bluntly reject an answer. If it's incorrect, ask what others think or ask the person for clarification.
11. End each class with a time of prayer, giving participants an opportunity to share with God whatever is on their heart.
12. In the first session, if the group members don't know each other, have each person *briefly* introduce themselves. Keep it short so you have time for the Bible Study.

Note: the questions in parenthesis, for example (2b) on Chapter 1, below, can be left out if time is short.

Chapter 1—Finding Joy's Door

Objective: To discover where true joy resides and the importance of rejoicing in the Lord.

Bring a padlock with several different keys, but only one which opens the lock. Give the keys to various people. You keep the right key. Pass the padlock and have each person try to open it. Verbalize how you must have the right key to open the padlock—like you need the right key to unlock joy in your life. Talk about what the group thinks will unlock joy.

Day 1:   Questions 1a-b, 2, 3, 3a, 4

Day 2:   Questions 1 and 2: Discuss how true joy can only be found by trusting Jesus. Encourage anyone who hasn't accepted Jesus as Savior to talk to you after class.

Day 2:   Questions (2b), 3-4, 6

Day 3:   Questions 1, (2), 3, 6

Day 4:   Questions 1, 2-6: Ask, "What has God done and given to you that fill you with joy?

Day 5:   Questions 1-3

Chapter 2—Knowing God Unlocks Joy

Objective: To grow to know God in a deeper, more personal way.

Lead a discussion on how intimacy is developed with another person. Which of these means can we use to know God better?

Day 1:   Questions la-b, 2, 2a, 3a, 4, (5), 5a

Day 2:   Question 2: Ask, "Which results have you experienced and how?"

Day 2:   Questions (3), 5-6

Day 3:   Questions 3, 3a, (4)

Day 4:   Questions (1) 2-3, 5

Day 5:   Questions (1), 2-3, (4), 5

End with a time of praise using the characteristics of God listed in day 3, questions 2 and 3.

Chapter 3—God's Word Reveals Joy

Objective: To see the importance of spending time in God's Word daily and the joy the Scriptures can bring.

Have the group recall the excitement of receiving a love letter. Was it left unopened for days or read eagerly? The Bible is our love letter from God. Ask, "Do we approach it with the same eagerness?"

Day 1:   Questions la-b: Have several share methods they use to begin their time in the Word.

Day 1:   Questions 2a-b, 4a-c

Day 2:   Questions 1a-b, 2a-b, (3), 4

Day 3:   Questions (1a, 3b, 4, 6)

Day 4:   Questions 1b, 2-5

Day 5:   Questions (1), 2-3, (4)

Chapter 4—Trust Releases Joy

Objective: To encourage more trust in God in our daily lives and to see the vital link connecting trust and joy.

Read Proverbs 3:5-6 together. Discuss the importance of trusting God completely. Ask, "How can we trust God with all our hearts? How do you practically trust God, especially during trials?"

Day 1:   Questions la-b, 2: Discuss how trust unlocks joy.

Day 1:   Questions (4), 5b

Day 2:   Questions 1, (2-3), 4-6, 7, 7b

Day 3:   Questions 1, 5, 7

Day 4:   Questions 1a, (2b), 3, (4)

Day 5:   Question 2

Divide the group into pairs. Challenge members to quote the verse each chose to memorize and to share an area in which it is hard for them to trust God. Pray in pairs about these issues.

Chapter 5— The Holy Spirit Releases Joy

Objective: To understand in what ways the Holy Spirit gives us joy and get to know Him in new ways.

Discuss storms the Holy Spirit has used in peoples lives--either literal or figurative.

Day 1:   Questions 1a-b, 2b-c, 3, (4)

Day 2:   Questions 1b-c, g, 2b, 3, (4)

Day 3:   Questions 1d-f, 2c, 4b, 6

Day 4:   Questions 1b-c, 2, 3g, 5

Day 5:   Questions 1-4

End with a time of prayer, asking the Holy Spirit to reveal Himself to each of you in new and fresh ways.

Chapter 6—Obedience Restores Joy

Objective: To examine our own lives to see if any disobedience exists and to deal with it in order to discover joy.

Discuss Brad and Jean from the narrative. What hindered their joy? What should they have done differently?

Begin with question 4, day 5, to review all previous keys.

Day 1:   Questions la-b, (2), 2a, 2c, 3a-b, (4, 6, 8), 9a, 9c

Day 2:   Questions 2, (4), 5a

Day 3:   Questions la-b, 2c, 3, 3b, 6

Day 4:   Questions (2b), 3b, 6

Day 5:   Questions 1, 3

Chapter 7—Prayer Maintains Joy

Objective: To learn more about prayer and encourage a greater and more effective personal prayer life. To see how prayer can maintain joy.

Begin by having one or two share from question 11, day 1.

Day 1:   Questions la-b, 5,6a, 7b, (8)

Day 2:   Questions 2a, 5, 8-9: Discuss fasting. What are the purposes and results? What are some ways to fast? What results has anyone experienced from fasting?

Day 3:   Questions 3, 4, (5a-b), 7b, 8

Day 4:   Questions 1, 5

Day 4:   Question 6: Talk about the answers and principles for prayer gleaned from the passages.

Day 4:   Questions 7, 8a, 8c

Day 5:   Questions (1), 2, 3

Chapter 8—Worship Unleashes Joy

Objective: To discover how to praise and worship God more and to see how worship both brings joy and is also an expression of our joy.

Discuss how an earthly king's subjects honor him. How is our worship of God similar? What are the differences?

Read Psalm 100:2 (NIV) and discuss.

Day 1:   Questions 1a-b, 3.

Day 1:   Question 4: Have the group share about their personal worship time. What works and doesn't work for them? In what ways can they improve it?

Day 1:   Question 8

Day 2:   Questions (1, 2), 3b, 5-6

Day 4:   Questions 1-2, (5)

Day 5:   Questions 2, (4)

End with a time of praise and worship. If desired, individuals could read their responses to question 4, day 5.

Chapter 9—Trials Build Joy

Objective: To understand the close relationship between suffering and joy. To discover purposes, results, examples, and responses to trials that will bring joy.

Discuss the relationship between trials and joy. What is God's view of how these should relate to each other? How does that compare with our view?

Day 1:   Questions la-b, 2a-c, 3, (6), 9

Day 2:   Questions 2a-b, 3a-b, 4, (6)

Day 3:   Questions (1-3), 5

Day 3:   Question 6: Discuss Habakkuk's situation and his response. Ask, "How does his example encourage or challenge you?"

Day 4:   Questions 2, (3-6), 7

Day 5:   Questions 1, (2), 3, 5

Chapter 10—Friendships Increase Joy

Objective: To understand that relationships to other Christians can both bring joy to us personally and give joy to others.

Ask them to share what kinds of things they do with family and friends to build joy. Review the ideas mentioned in the narrative and ask which bring the most joy to them.

Day 1:   Questions la-b, 2c-d, (3), 4-5

Day 2:   Questions 2-3, 6

Day 3:   Questions (1), 3, 5

Day 4:   Questions 2a, (3-4), 6

Day 5:   Questions 1a-b, 2

Have several share their memory verses and hints that help them memorize Scripture. Mention www.365NamesofGod.com has a page on "Ideas for Hiding God's Word in Your Heart."

Chapter 11—An Attitude Check Unbinds Joy

Objective: To understand that what's going on inside is more important than our circumstances for determining the extent of our joy. Also, to help each person look realistically at his or her own joy-killers.

Review and discuss the three steps given in the narrative for experiencing the full joy Jesus intended. Ask, "Which of these helped you most?"

Day 1: Questions la-b, 2, 2a-b, 3a-c, 6-7, (9a-b)

Day 2: Question 2

Day 2: Question 3: Have someone share how he/she began dealing with a weakness this week using these steps.

Day 3: Questions 1, (2), 3-8, 10

Day 4: Questions 1b, (4-5), 6a, 7

Day 5: Questions (1), 3, (4)

Chapter 12—Gratitude Encourages Joy

Objective: To recognize how gratitude encourages joy in both the giver and the receiver. It also is an expression of joy.

Discuss the reciprocal relationship between gratitude and joy—joy brings gratitude and gratitude brings joy. Have someone share a personal example of this.

Day 1:   Questions 1-3, 5, 6a-b

Day 2:   Questions 2, 3, (5), 7-9

Day 3:   Questions (1), 2, 4, 5, (7-8), 10-11

Day 4:   Questions 1, 4

Day 5:   Questions 1-4

End with a time of prayer with each person thanking God for one or two things for which they are grateful. These could be from their list in question 7, day 1.

Chapter 13—Review Cements Joy

Objective: To review all the keys to joy so the truths will be cemented into their minds and hearts. To encourage continued application of each key.

Suggestion: Take two weeks if possible to study this chapter, since there is so much information to review.

Ask who can list all the keys to joy from memory. Or list them as a group.

Day 1:   Questions la-b, 2, 3

Discuss questions a, b, d (and possibly e) for each chapter. Also, talk about the journal questions, if time.

Day 5:   Questions 3, 5, 6

Note: at the end of this book are two other books that can be—and have been—used in small groups and Bible studies.

About Us

Gaylyn Williams is...

- The director of Relationship Resources, Inc., since 1999

- Passionate about empowering people in their lives and relationships with God, themselves and others

- A published author with sixteen books

- A magazine writer with numerous published articles in various magazines

- An international motivational speaker and seminar trainer

- Mother of two grown sons

- A former missionary with Wycliffe Bible Translators from 1972 to 1992

- A former missionary with The Navigators from 1997-1999

Dr. Ken Williams:

- He and his wife Bobbie began their ministry with Wycliffe Bible Translators in 1957. They first served among the Chuj people of Guatemala, completing a translation of the New Testament, as well as founding a Bible Institute, literacy work, and medical clinics.

- In the early 1970's Ken began providing care and counseling for cross-cultural workers. Ken earned his Ph.D. in Human Behavior, and he and Bobbie continued in this ministry with WBT for 22 years, counseling thousands of missionaries worldwide.

- Ken came to realize that many of the difficult issues addressed in counseling could be avoided if believers received effective training in interpersonal relationships and managing stress. This was accompanied by Ken's deep conviction that healthy, godly relationships are best built and sustained by living out God's word.

- In 1987 Ken began to develop training programs for workers in Christian ministries, especially mission organizations.

About the Publisher

Relationship Resources...

- Facilitates growth for believers and not-yet-believers in their relationships with God, themselves and other people

- Provides practical, biblical, interactive workshops and materials designed to empower and equip individuals and groups in their lives, work and ministries

- Trains and mentors facilitators to provide their workshops for other groups

- Gained IRS nonprofit status in 1999

- Began as a concept in 1970 with Ken Williams training missionaries

- Offers workshops on many topics, including:

  o Keys to Transform Your Relationships
  o Reconcilable Differences
  o Sharpen Your Interpersonal Skills
  o Surprised by Joy
  o De-Stress Your Life

For more information, go to www.RelationshipResources.org.

**To get a free sample of Gaylyn's latest book,
The Surprising Joy of Exploring God's Heart
email us at Freesample@365NamesofGod.com.**

See the following section for more information or go to www.365NamesofGod.com.

Other Books By The Authors

These books are available on www.RRbooks.org. Use the discount code "KeysToJoy" in the shopping cart to get a 25% discount on either book.

All Stressed Up and Everywhere to Go!
Solutions to De-Stressing Your Life
and Recovering Your Sanity

By Gaylyn R. Williams and Ken Williams Ph.D

From the daily hassles to the catastrophic events, this book will empower you to successfully de-stress your life and recover your sanity. You'll discover easy –to-use skills enabling you to gain greater freedom from life's ups and downs.

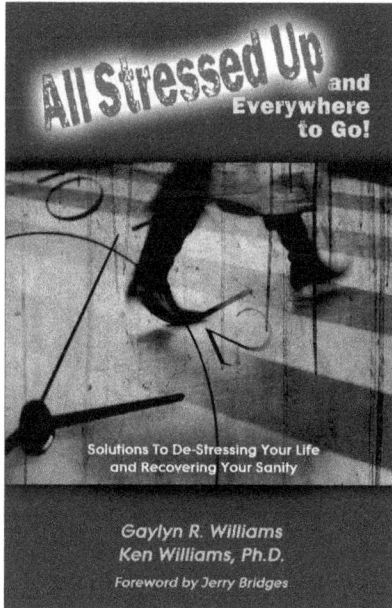

In today's fast-paced, overworked world, stress is all around us: the economy, finances, raising children, health, job, school, family or lack of it, elderly parents, divorce, tragedy, debt, death, and conflict.

This is not an ordinary book about stress.

This unique workbook contains practical, biblical tools for attaining spiritual, emotional, physical, and interpersonal balance. It is filled with powerful personal stories to illustrate principles, thought-provoking questions for individual or group study, Bible studies, self-assessments, and easy-to-apply strategies to develop a balanced lifestyle.

As you explore the timeless connection between the biblical principles and this practical, life-enhancing approach, you'll gain valuable solutions to cope with your own stress, as well as help friends and family.

These powerful strategies have been proven worldwide. Over 20,000 believers in 80 plus countries have learned these life-changing skills. Ken and Gaylyn first tested them in their own lives and continue to use them on a regular basis.

Rather than writing from a clinical perspective—although Dr. Williams, with his PhD in Human Behavior, could do that—they honestly share their personal experiences having each dealt with numerous major and minor stresses. They have trained people in Christian organizations in these methods for twenty-five years. Now they are available to you.

Available in Paperback, PDF, Kindle and Epub

The Surprising Joy of Exploring God's Heart: A Daily Adventure with 365 of His Names

By Gaylyn R. Williams

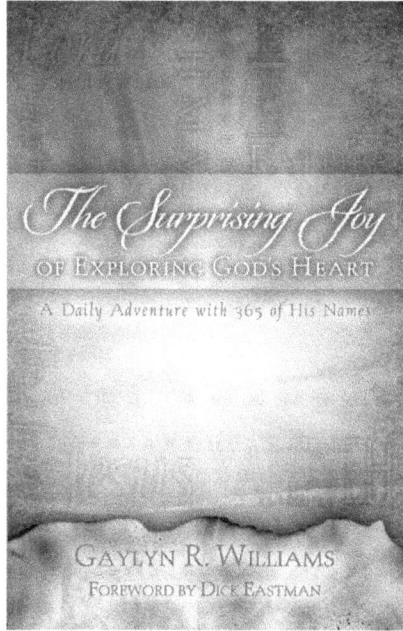

Embark on a Life-Changing Adventure!

Do you long to fall deeper in love with God? Would you like to come into His presence in new and fresh ways? In as little as five minutes a day, enhance your intimacy with God as you explore His names.

This powerful, daily devotional and journal will help you:

- Discover new insights into your awesome God

- Experience comfort, strength and hope from understanding God's character

- Expand your vision for God's power, majesty and greatness

- Enjoy a growing passion for God through praise and worship

- Transform your prayer life and strengthen your faith

This unique treasure contains 365 names of God directly from the Bible. Uncover daily encouragement as you dig deeper into who God is and how He relates to you personally.

Individuals, couples, families and small groups can use this simple, yet powerful tool to climb to new heights in your relationship with God and others. You'll be forever changed as you get to know God in new ways.

Available in Paperback, PDF, Kindle and Epub

References

Aldrich, Joe (1985) "Joy, The Illusive Fruit," Retrieved June 25, 2012 from
http://www.navpress.com/magazines/archives/article.aspx?id=14085
(Originally published in Discipleship Journal September | October 1985 issue)

Bridges, Jerry (1989) Trusting God Even When Life Hurts, Colorado Springs, CO:
NavPress.

Bridges, Jerry (1996) The Practice of Godliness, Colorado Springs, CO: NavPress.

Hansel, Tim (1985) You Gotta Keep Dancin', Elgin, IL: David C. Cook Publishing Co.

Miller, Calvin, (1983) Taste of Joy, Downers Grove, IL: Intervarsity Press

Piper, John   (2003) Desiring God, Portland, OR: Multnomah Publishers

Voskamp, Ann (2011) One Thousand Gifts, Grand Rapids, MI: Zondervan

www.ingramcontent.com/pod-product-compliance
Lightning Source LLC
LaVergne TN
LVHW011230080426
835509LV00005B/422